CASPIAN GAS

The Former Soviet South project is sponsored by:

- A. Meredith Jones & Co. Ltd.
- British American Tobacco
- BG plc
- The British Petroleum Company plc
- ENI S.p.A.
- Mobil Oil Company Ltd
- Shell International Petroleum Company Ltd
- Statoil

Series editor: Edmund Herzig
Head, Russia and Eurasia Programme: Roy Allison

The Royal Institute of International Affairs is an independent body which promotes the rigorous study of international questions and does not express opinions of its own. The opinions expressed in this publication are the responsibility of the author.

FORMER SOVIET SOUTH PROJECT

CASPIAN GAS

OTTAR SKAGEN

THE ROYAL INSTITUTE OF
INTERNATIONAL AFFAIRS
Russia and Eurasia Programme

CONTENTS

Tables

ABOUT THE AUTHOR

Ottar Skagen is currently project manager in the Gas Business Development division of Statoil. From 1993 to 1996 he worked in the International Energy Agency, concentrating on Caspian, Ukrainian, Polish and Baltic oil and gas issues. Before joining the IEA he spent five years as a member of Statoil's Corporate Strategy Development staff specializing in global oil and gas market analysis and scenario planning. Earlier work experience includes a period in the Norwegian Petroleum Directorate, four years as a country risk analysis in GIEK (an affiliate of the Norwegian Ministry of Trade) and stints as a journalist with Norwegian newspapers and radio.

ACKNOWLEDGMENTS

I would like to thank Edmund Herzig and Roy Allison of the Royal Institute of International Affairs for inviting me to write this paper, the RIIA study group participants who commented on the first draft, former colleagues and friends in the IEA, my wife Lena and baby Andreas for their patience during the preparation process.

October 1997   Ottar Skagen

ABBREVIATIONS

AzPF	Azerbaijan Popular Front
bcm	Billion cubic metres
CBR	Central Bank of Russia
CFE	Conventional Forces in Europe
CHG	Council of Heads of Government
CHS	Council of Heads of State
CICA	Conference on Interaction and Confidence-Building Measures in Asia
CIS	Commonwealth of Independent States
CMD	Council of Ministers of Defence
CMFA	Council of Ministers of Foreign Affairs
CSC	Collective Security Council
EAU	Eurasian Union
EBRD	European Bank for Reconstruction and Development
ECO	Economic Cooperation Organization
E&D	Exploration and development
E&P	Exploration and production
FDI	Foreign direct investment
FSS	Former Soviet South
FSU	Former Soviet Union
IMF	International Monetary Fund
ISEC	Inter-State Economic Committee
JCS	Joint Chiefs of Staff
JV	Joint venture
NACC	North Atlantic Cooperation Council
NATO	North Atlantic Treaty Organization
OSCE	Organization for Security and Cooperation in Europe
PfP	Partnership for Peace
PSA	Production-sharing agreement
SMCC	Staff for Military Cooperation and Coordination
START	Strategic Arms Reduction Talks
tcm	Trillion cubic metres
UNCTAD	United Nations Conference on Trade and Development
WTO	World Trade Organization

SUMMARY

The Caspian former Soviet Union (FSU) republics that are blessed with petroleum resources not only have the potential to become world-class exporters; they could also produce much more gas than they currently do. The resources are there, non-associated gas production costs are thought not to be higher than those prevailing in, say, parts of the Middle East, and some of the oilfields under development or slated for development contain a lot of associated gas. Political and legal operating conditions for foreign companies seem to be improving.

In some Caspian states, gas consumption amounts to more than two-thirds of total primary energy consumption, and most countries in the area intend to further increase the gas share of their energy use – to free up oil for exports, because gas-based electricity generation is more efficient than other thermal generation, to bolster the competitiveness of their energy-intensive industries, and for environmental reasons. However, the potential for growth in Caspian gas production is much bigger than that for growth in regional consumption, implying a potential for strong growth in gas exports.

Currently, most Caspian gas is consumed within the region, the only major exception being Turkmenistan's troubled exports to Ukraine. As the Turkmen, Uzbek, Kazak and Azeri gas industries came into being as affiliates of the Russian gas industry, before 1991 no one thought about building export pipelines directly from the Caspian area to non-FSU markets and since 1991 those who have called for the building of such lines have had a hard time attracting finance. The Caspian FSU republics remain dependent on Gazprom for their gas exports outside the FSU.

Possible export markets for Caspian gas include Turkey, Europe, South Asia, China and conceivably Japan in addition to the rest of the FSU. Nearly everywhere gas consumption is increasing. However, established producers/exporters stand ready to supply the bulk of incremental demand, and the field of new producers hoping to capture markets shares keeps growing, with certain gas-rich Middle Eastern and North African countries arguably in the lead in terms of their ability to compete on total supply costs including transportation costs. This does not mean that the Caspian gas producers will not manage to secure footholds in solvent export markets. But the perception that Caspian gas exports are constrained only by the current lack of independent export pipelines and will skyrocket as and when this problem is dealt with could prove too optimistic.

The purpose of this paper is to shed some light on the factors that will shape the Caspian area's development as a gas-producing area. Where the level of precision is found wanting it could be because the information is not yet publicly available or does not exist at all. Also, as writing on the Caspian area is very much like shooting at a moving target, undoubtedly bits and pieces of information will be outdated very quickly. Hopefully the gist of the text will prove a little more durable.

Map 1: Oil and gas basins in the Caspian region

Map 2: Existing and proposed gas pipelines in the Caspian region

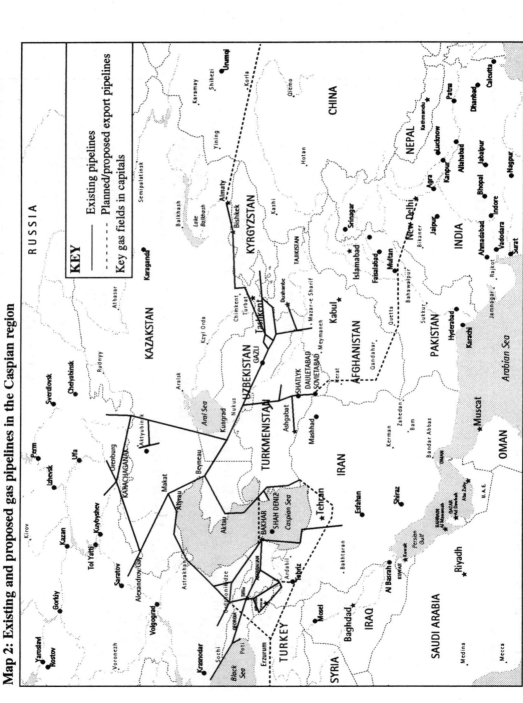

1 INTRODUCTION

Since the collapse of the former Soviet Union (FSU), the petroleum resources of Central Asia and the Caucasus have attracted continual and strong interest not only from the owners of the resources, i.e., the governments around the Caspian Sea, but also from politicians in the OECD area concerned about their countries' future energy supply and about the geopolitics of the Caspian area, from various Russian quarters, from Western oil and engineering companies chasing contracts and of course – as a result of all the hustling and bustling – from the international media.

For various reasons, Caspian[1] oil has received more coverage than has the area's gas. Azeri and Kazak oil could – if either Russian export pipelines were made available or independent pipelines put in place – be produced and marketed easily and profitably. It could also, under plausible assumptions on trends in world oil markets, make a difference to oil price developments and thus to oil companies' financial results and countries' trade balances. Consequently, Western companies and governments alike have evident interests in the area's oil. On the other hand, the European gas market, on which Central Asian and Caucasian gas authorities pin their strongest export hopes, remains hard to break into, and the world gas market is commonly seen as facing the risk of oversupply rather than the opposite. Huge Caspian gas development projects with long lead times would seem to represent higher commercial risks than comparatively sized oil projects, and European governments may attach less importance to facilitating Caspian gas exports than oil exports. For these reasons there have been fewer spectacular gas projects, with fewer companies, less money and lower political stakes involved than in oil.

However, perceptions could change. More countries could come to see Central Asian and Caucasian gas as interesting in the context of a diversification of imports. Perhaps more important in attracting attention to the issue, the political implications of supporting or not supporting Caspian gas could be further accentuated. The tug-of-war over oil export routes out of the Caspian area quickly became intertwined with the

---

[1]Although only three of the eight FSU republics – Armenia, Azerbaijan, Georgia, Kazakstan, Kyrgyzstan, Tajikistan, Turkmenistan and Uzbekistan – whose gas affairs are the subject of this paper have Caspian coastlines, we will for the sake of simplicity refer to all of them as Caspian countries.

1

international competition for control or influence over the Caucasian and Central Asian countries, and with the question of securing their real economic and political independence. The barriers to a realization of the gas potential of the area are partly political, too, and increased gas exports would also bolster the area's independence.

As discussions have hitherto centred on one country, Turkmenistan, whose government has proceeded hesitantly with economic reforms, shied away from political liberalization and been reluctant to invite foreign companies in on big projects – that is, has not behaved in the best way to invoke general Western interest and sympathy – the politics of Caspian gas may not have seemed so urgent. Now, however, both Turkmenistan and Uzbekistan are taking steps to attract foreign investment, Azerbaijan sees itself as a future gas exporter and Kazakstan, currently more concerned with supplying domestic gas needs than with exports, could rethink its priorities if offshore gas deposits turn out to be large. In short, the stakes could become higher.

The importance of gas to the Central Asian and Caucasian republics themselves is evident. Tens of millions of people in the area, and countless enterprises, rely on gas as their main fuel. Improvements in supply regularity – based on improved payment regularity – would greatly facilitate economic development. An upswing in gas exports outside the area would impact strongly on the trade and government balances and budgets of the exporting countries, provided, of course, that exports were paid for. As will be argued, total Caspian area gas exports (i.e., exports net of intraregional flows) could approach 100 bcm a year in 12–15 years' time if markets are found, foreign investment in gas exploration and development (E&D) takes off, and current export pipeline constraints are lifted as quickly as technically and economically feasible. If the exporters receive, say, an average of US$50 per 1,000 cubic metres (cu.m) exported, aggregate revenues could amount to $4.8 billion a year by 2010. (The Caspian states' combined total export revenues in 1995 amounted to about $12 billion.)

It is certainly possible to argue a scenario where the conditions for a rapid increase in exports do not materialize – leaving Central Asian and Caucasian gas production limited to supplying regional demand and bits and pieces of Ukrainian and other FSU demand – but it is still interesting to examine more closely the potentials and the factors that will determine the republics' degree of success as gas exporters. Moreover, output growth rates do not have to increase to their geological and technical limits to make a difference to local economies. Even modest increases in Turkmenistan's gas production would send strong growth impulses into the Turkmen economy. Even a partial restoration of Azerbaijan's gas production to the levels of the late 1980s would free up oil substituted for gas in the power sector, and allow industry laid idle by gas shortages to restart operations. Even minor moves towards gas self-sufficiency for the republics currently producing little or no gas would serve to improve their trade balances and help them in their negotiations with suppliers.

2 GAS RESERVES

Estimates of the Central Asian and Caucasian republics' oil and gas reserves vary across sources owing to:

- differences in reserves and resource classification systems, and consequent misunderstandings as to the meaning of figures;
- a lack of information and diverging interpretations of the information that exists;
- the political agendas of some sources of information.

It is probable that semantics now play a decreasing role, and the unevenness and complexity of reserves and resource data and the politicization of reserves reporting increasing roles, in explaining variations.

Estimates also change more from one year to the next than can be explained by new discoveries and production; the pool of geological and reservoir information is growing, warranting sometimes major revisions of conclusions. Parts of the area have not been explored at all, and those parts that have been explored generally need to be revisited with state-of-the-art exploration methods and technology. Western companies are gaining access to the area, and seismic surveys are being conducted, but many prospects have not yet been drilled.

At the lower end of the ranges formed by the estimates of individual republics' reserves are the official Russian estimates based on evaluations carried out during the 1980s. Russian geologists – e.g., those in VNIIgaz, a subsidiary of Gazprom – argue that the amount of exploration carried out under the auspices of national authorities since the break-up of the FSU, and the number and size of new discoveries made since then, generally do not justify the dramatic upward adjustments of estimates made by some national authorities. Russian experts consider – at least officially – Central Asian and Caucasian gas reserves to be in the range of 6.5–7 trillion cubic metres (tcm).

At the higher end are the Caspian governments' own estimates. According to them, gas reserves in the area amount to 30–40 tcm.[2] This official optimism is understandable.

---

[2] Some of these estimates, although reported as reserves estimates, are probably in reality total resource estimates.

Playing up one's assets and longer-term potential is part and parcel of the competition for foreign investment, and countries in the positions of the Central Asian and Caucasian republics cannot be blamed for exploiting the uncertainties that exist. Moreover, governments striving to build national identity and pride, and trying to contain unrest in the face of severe economic and social hardships, cannot be blamed for riding roughshod over probability distributions to nurture the hope of a brighter future.

By and large, Western company and independent experts occupy the middle ground. Thus, Petroconsultants – a Geneva-based consultancy – estimate the eight Central Asian and Caucasian republics' combined proven and probable gas reserves at 9.85 tcm (see Table 1). To provide some perspective, this is 15–20% of estimated total FSU reserves and less than half of estimated Iranian reserves, but 15–20% above the proven reserves of North America, including Mexico, and 40–80% (depending on source) above all of Europe's proven reserves.

Table 1: Natural gas reserves, reserves to production ratios[a] (bcm, years)

	Reserves	R/p ratios[b]
Armenia	—	—
Azerbaijan	598.82	95
Georgia	6.46	—
Kazakstan	2,225.87	525
Kyrgyzstan	25.61	850
Tajikistan	15.65	520
Turkmenistan	4,353.36	123
Uzbekistan	2,624.33	55
Total	9,850.10	105

Source: Petroconsultants.

[a] The estimates include A plus B plus C_1 category reserves in Russian terminology, i.e., proven reserves and some probable reserves in Western terminology.
[b] The ratio between the proven gas (oil) reserves and the current annual gas (oil) production of a country is a dubious illustration of the size of its reserves. A gas r/p ratio of, say, 100 years does not mean that the country can continue producing at the current level for 100 years without discovering and developing more fields; output would start to decline and reach the threshold for economic production long before reserves were fully exhausted. At the same time, an r/p ratio of 10 years does not mean that the country will cease to be a gas producer in 10 years' time, only that companies have no incentives to prove up more reserves. However, r/p ratios are quoted everywhere and can be used for comparison purposes, which is why they are reported here.

Azerbaijan owes its oil and gas reserves to the *South Caspian* basin (see map 1) which extends from Georgia across Azeri territory and the Caspian Sea to western Turkmenistan. The biggest fields have been located in a narrow structural zone which runs along the northern boundary of the basin from the Apsheron peninsula north of Baku into the Azeri section of the Caspian Sea.[3]

As indicated, Caspian state authorities' estimates of their countries' proven and probable on- and offshore reserves generally exceed estimates by Western sources. Thus, the president of the State Oil Company of Azerbaijan (Socar) holds that gas reserves under Azeri jurisdiction amount to some 7,000 billion cubic metres (bcm).

The bulk of **Kazakstan's** oil and gas reserves are thought to be located in the *North Caspian* basin, which includes the part of the Caspian Sea north of the 45th parallel, northwest Kazakstan, and also Astrakhan and much of Kalmykia in Russia. In the late 1970s three so-called supergiant fields – Tengiz and Karachaganak in Kazakstan and Astrakhan in Russia – were discovered in this basin. Since then, however, exploration results have mostly been disappointing. The US Geological Survey nevertheless characterizes the basin as still at an immature stage of exploration. Discoveries could also be made in a number of other basins: the *North Ustyurt* basin including the Buzachi peninsula protruding into the Caspian some 100 km south of Tengiz; the *Middle Caspian* basin extending across the Caspian Sea from the 45th parallel in the north to the Apsheron Sill in the south and including the Mangyshlak peninsula south of the Buzachi peninsula; and the *South Turgay* and *Chu-Sarysu* basins in central Kazakstan.

Azerbaijan shares the South Caspian basin with **Turkmenistan**. Discoveries have been made also in the Turkmen part of the Apsheron Sill, and the string of fields running eastward from Cheleken and then southward along the Turkmen coast tracks the eastern boundary of the basin. Most of the gas reserves, however, are located in the *Amu Darya* basin in the central and eastern parts of the country.

A Western geophysical company working for the Turkmen government estimates the republic's probable gas reserves at about 16,000 bcm. The government itself last year put reserves at more than 21,000 bcm. Other observers dismiss such figures as wishful thinking.

Russian researchers in VNIIgaz appear to stick to the results of the last formal evaluation of Turkmenistan's gas reserves, carried out in 1988.[4] They now put initial reserves at 9,400 bcm and remaining reserves, after cumulative production of 1,560

---

[3]We will refer to national sectors of the Caspian Sea as if a legal regime for the sea had been agreed whereby the littoral states can decide unilaterally on resource development projects within their sectors; such a regime, however, has not yet been established.
[4]*Eastern Bloc Energy*, April 1997.

bcm, at 7,840 bcm, of which 2,700 bcm are classified as proved, probable and possible and the remainder as forecast, i.e., speculative. Besides pointing out that since 1990 little exploration has taken place and that new discoveries have been small, they note that the bulk of speculative gas is likely to be located at great depths in complex formations with anomalously high pressure, and to contain high contents of hydrogen sulphide, rendering production much more expensive than for the proven gas.

Turkmenistan shares the Amu Darya basin with **Uzbekistan**, and most of the latter's oil and gas reserves are located in a strip of territory some 100 km wide on its of the border. Other basins where discoveries have been made are the North Ustyurt basin mentioned above, which extends from western Uzbekistan into Kazakstan; the *Fergana* basin extending from eastern Uzbekistan into Tajikistan and Kyrgyzstan; and the *South Tajik* basin extending from southern Uzbekistan into Tajikistan.

Uzbekneftegaz geologists estimate Uzbekistan's proven and potential natural gas reserves at 1,940 bcm – more than twice the levels suggested by Petroconsultants – and put potential reserves at about 7,200 bcm.

Oil and gas discoveries have also been made in the other Central Asian and Caucasian republics – **Kyrgyzstan**, **Tajikistan**, **Armenia** and **Georgia**. Recoverable reserves appear modest and observers see none of them developing into significant producers, let alone exporters. However, if foreign investors were given the right incentives, fuel self-sufficiency ratios could increase to an extent that would matter locally, lessening fuel import payment burdens and reducing the impact of fuel import irregularities.

As mentioned, the Fergana basin straddles both Kyrgyzstan and Tajikistan, and minor shares of gas discovered in this basin by the late 1980s were located in these republics. Their combined recoverable gas reserves are put at about 40 bcm, as Table 1 shows.

On the other side of the Caspian Sea, the Armenian Ministry of Fuel and Energy hired a team of European experts in 1995 to evaluate the geology and oil and gas potential of the country with a view to enticing exploration by foreign companies. The experts concluded that Armenia had too small a potential for the country to launch an exploration programme. The ministry nevertheless proceeded with its plans and divided the country into five large blocks to be offered to companies in an international tender.

Georgia is an established, although small oil producer, and US geologists who have surveyed its oilfields and on-and offshore prospects think – according to Interfax – that there may be up to 300 million tonnes or 2.2 billion barrels of oil waiting to be discovered off the Georgian Black Sea coast, and almost as much onshore. However, gas reserves are apparently thought to be insignificant.

3 GAS INDUSTRY DEVELOPMENTS AND GAS PRODUCTION

The Caspian republics have much in common: their land-lockedness, their history as periphery within the Soviet Union and their more recent history as patchily developed and generally inefficient economies caught in a web of transition problems. The differences between them are no less striking, however, and will probably become more pronounced as they emerge as 'normal' countries with normal economic and political problems. They vary enormously in terms of size, population, demographic and ethnic composition, natural resource endowments, economic structure, religion, culture and – intertwined with many of these features – attitude towards economic and political reform.

The gas industries of those republics that produce gas also share a number of characteristics. Until 1991 they were local divisions of the Soviet gas industry, taking orders on most issues except day-to-day operations from Moscow, receiving inputs from all over the Union according to the hierarchy of plans for the industry, implementing major investment projects with the aid of experts dispatched by the centre, producing to meet plan targets, supplying local customers according to instructions and seeing gas destined for other parts of the Union or for exports without having to worry about marketing or payments. Independence thus landed them with a number of tasks for which they were totally unprepared. Thus, when input deliveries failed to appear because there was no one to plan them any longer, it took time to set up purchase departments able to organize tenders and negotiate deals, and when the flow of funds from the centre dried up, it took time even to get started down the road towards efficiency improvements, price reform, metering of consumption and strict payment collection, all essential for financial independence.

Another common feature is bloated and generally inefficient organizations reflecting the history of enterprises as bureaucracies and monopolies, and an unwillingness, on the part of the enterprise or the government, or both, to deal with the requirements of the day by spinning off ancillary functions and shedding staff.

Problems often feed upon themselves. Like most major FSU industries, the Caspian gas industries suffer under mountains of inter-enterprise and inter-republican debts. Like the gas industries of the other FSU republics, those of the Caspian states have a hard time making ordinary people and decision-makers give up the perception of gas as an essentially free good, priced at below supply costs and paid for (if at all)

7

according to consumption-insensitive norms. Thus, although inter-republican gas export prices have increased, the exporting countries have not seen similar increases in gas payments. Additionally, though the oil and gas sector may be hard up, it may still be seen as a cash cow by the government, and taxed to the bone. Thus, companies may not be left with enough money to keep fields from declining prematurely and to deal with pipeline corrosion and leaks, let alone to replace produced reserves through E&D and to build new infrastructure.

Government and industry responses to problems vary across countries, however. Some of the Caspian gas industries are only now, after more than five years as independent organizations, embarking on reforms. By early 1997 all the Caspian republics professed to welcome foreign investment in the petroleum sector, but some are greeting foreign companies with greater reservations than others; the understanding of private companies' risk-reward thinking, and of the international competition for investment funds, is not equally well developed all over the area. On the same note, attitudes to privatization of oil and gas companies range from almost total rejection to an apparent willingness to float the bulk of shares in each and every company involved in petroleum production and transportation.

In this chapter we will look at the ways the gas industries in each of the Caspian FSU republics are set up, gas sector reforms, legal and other institutional framework conditions for foreign investment, and recent and anticipated gas production developments.

Turkmenistan

As noted, Turkmenistan possesses 44% of the Caspian republics' gas reserves as estimated by Western sources, and an even higher share according to the Turkmen authorities' own estimates. Currently Turkmenistan is only second among Central Asian and Caucasian gas producers, but in the late 1980s the republic was the fourth biggest producer in the world with an output of almost 90 bcm a year. Demand for Turkmen gas has dropped as a result of domestic, regional and FSU-wide economic contraction and inter-republican payment problems, and because Turkmenistan has been completely cut off from export markets outside the FSU. The republic could, however, regain its position as a world-class gas producer. That will depend primarily on market and access factors, but also on domestic political developments.

The Turkmen petroleum industry had seen little real reform by mid-1997. Two reorganizations had taken place, but apparently they were driven more by personal rivalry and power politics than by a desire to streamline oil and gas operations. Turkmen petroleum authorities by and large do not even bother to pay lip service to the principles of transparent decision-making and accountability. Private foreign participation in exploration and production (E&P) remains very limited.

8

Between 1991 and 1993 the Turkmen petroleum industry comprised a number of independent 'concerns' such as Turkmengazprom which was responsible for gas production and Turkmentransgaz which operated the republic's gas pipelines. These entities were successors of the Turkmen divisions of the Soviet petroleum industry. In 1993, however, the president issued a resolution abolishing all of them and putting their component enterprises under the supervision of a Ministry of Oil and Gas. The ministry thus came to supervise – among other entities – three gas production associations operating on a regional basis outside the area of the republic's single oil-producing association, five gas distribution organizations and various geophysical 'expeditions', building and construction units and service units.

This structure survived until July 1996 when President Niyazov issued a decree on the replacement of the Ministry of Oil and Gas by an integrated Ministry of the Oil and Gas Industry and Mineral Resources. This ministry is smaller and will be less powerful than its predecessor, since a number of the old ministry's companies and organizations have been transformed into three state concerns and two government corporations in charge of oil production, gas production, exploration etc., which themselves enjoy the status of ministries.

As noted, foreign companies have played marginal roles in the Turkmen oil and gas sector. For years only two partnerships between foreign companies and the Turkmen government were up and running, and both have been stormy. Bridas, an Argentinian company, in 1996 took legal action against the Turkmen government for having revoked its oil export licence, forcing the company to sell crude at a loss to a local refinery. The Turkmen authorities claim on their side that Bridas exploited its position as a firstcomer to independent Turkmenistan, tricking the inexperienced Turkmen negotiators into accepting an agreement that was unreasonably favourable to the company, and subsequently refusing to renegotiate this agreement. Larmag and Dragon, two other early entrants registered in the Netherlands and Ireland respectively, also were put under pressure as the government decided it had made too many concessions during initial negotiations. These companies have agreed to a revision of terms. Irrespective of the truth of the parties' conflicting stories, the experiences of these companies have tarnished the Turkmen government's reputation as a joint venture (JV) partner and helped keep other companies away.

However, in June 1996 Petronas of Malaysia signed a production-sharing agreement (PSA) with the Turkmen government; in February 1997 Mobil and Monument Oil & Gas signed an agreement with the government to negotiate a PSA for an area in western Turkmenistan; and a string of other companies including TPAO, Unocal, Delta, Itochu and the China National Petroleum Corporation are looking at E&P projects.

Russia, too, is eyeing Turkmenistan's resources – in 1995 the Turkmen government,

Gazprom and a US-based company with close links to Russian interests, Itera, formed the Turkemenrosgaz JV with a mandate extending from exploring for oil and gas on Turkmen territory to exporting Turkmen gas to the rest of – and possibly beyond – the FSU. Turkmenrosgaz was to buy gas at the Turkmen–Uzbek border, initially at US$42 per 1,000 cubic metres, resell it to Ukraine and other customers, handle transportation and collect payments.[5]

The Turkmen government has repeatedly announced international tenders for exploration and development rights offshore as well as onshore. In 1996 it made known that a tender for two sets of blocks covering the entire 72,000 square km Turkmen sector of the Caspian Sea was under preparation. Reserves in the area were estimated – by Turkmen geologists – at 4.8 trillion cubic metres of gas in addition to 3 billion tons of oil. Observers concluded that the Turkmens had finally come to side with the Azeris and the Kazaks in the conflict over the littoral states' right to manage the resources in their respective sectors of the Caspian Sea. Then, in November, a gathering of Caspian Sea littoral states' foreign ministers in Ashgabat resulted in a decision to set up a joint Russian–Iranian–Turkmen company to manage the extraction of hydrocarbons from the Caspian shelf outside a 45-mile coastal zone, and the plan to tender offshore blocks in the Turkmen sector was delayed pending agreement among all the littoral states on the partitioning issue. Observers saw a link between Turkmenistan's U-turn on this issue and a Russian U-turn on the question of granting Turkmenistan access to its export pipelines to Europe. During the first half of 1997 the Turkmen authorities strove mainly to interest foreign companies in rehabilitating the country's idle, partly depleted onshore oilfields. However, towards the middle of the year the Niyazov administration appeared to have accepted development of the resources under the seabed on a national-sector basis as a fact if not as a principle, while the Russian–Iranian–Turkmen company appeared to be in limbo.

Investment framework conditions

The cosmetic character of much of the reorganization of the oil and gas sector is but one expression of the fact that the Turkmen government has taken few and unconvincing shots at economic and political reform. Steps to liberalize prices in 1992 were hastily rolled back when their inflationary consequences became evident. The president has been reluctant to scrap welfare schemes such as heavy subsidization of basic foodstuffs and free supplies of water, gas and electricity to households,

---

[5] By mid-1997 news agencies reported that President Niyazov had signed a decree disbanding Turkmenrosgaz, claiming that the venture had not worked and was unlikely to do so in the future.

10

schemes launched in the belief that increasing gas revenues would flow into state coffers. Foreign trade is still conducted through centralized state trading organizations. The market value of the local currency, the manat, is a fraction of the official value. Privatization has hardly started – the entire private sector including spontaneously established home industries and informal market trading is thought to account for less than a fifth of GNP. Since 1995 some liberalization measures have been decided, but doubts persist as to when and how they will be implemented.

A law on foreign investment passed in May 1992 and amended in October 1993 contains a grandfathering clause affording protection from law amendments to the detriment of the investor for ten years after the registration of the venture, but no one has yet tried to invoke it. The profit tax rate is 25%, with exemptions for foreign partners in JVs until they have recovered their initial investments.

In principle, oil and gas resources may be exploited under a concession agreement, a subsurface licence or a PSA. In October 1993 a concessions law was passed, directed at foreign investment in a wide range of sectors including the petroleum sector. Concessions are to be granted on a 'competitive basis' with terms and conditions determined by the Council of Ministers. The law gives the state the right to a share of profits and the right to purchase the concession's output, and the concessionaire the exclusive right to use whatever is covered by the concession, the right to compensation in the event of cancellation of the concession, and the right to export shares, as stipulated in each agreement, of the output and hard-currency profits.

In May 1994 the government passed the Law on Subsurface Resources, providing for the granting of exploitation licences by tender or auction, and in January 1996 it adopted a model PSA – developed by the Ministry of Oil and Gas in cooperation with the Italian power industry holding company ENEL – to serve as a basis for future negotiations. The Ministry and ENEL have also developed draft laws on PSAs and on oil and gas, and a model exploration and development JV agreement. This development of new legislation was driven mainly by governmental dissatisfaction with the performance of existing deals and partnerships. Officials have frequently complained that foreign companies do not carry out promised investment programmes, and that they get away with it as their agreements render the government unable to compel them to fulfil their obligations.

According to the model PSA, agreements will be concluded for 25 years with the possibility of a ten-year extension. An agreement covering oil E&P but leading to a gas discovery will not entitle the investor to use the gas for anything but reinjection; producing and selling it will require a separate agreement. The draft model JV agreement generally limits the stake of foreign investors in a JV to 10–30%. Investors may obtain larger shares if they undertake to spend extraordinarily large sums on exploration. The draft stipulates the duration of E&P licences, and the investor's share of the profits; the latter will vary inversely in the range of 10–65% with the profitability of the project. Bonuses and royalties will depend on the level of production, with the range of royalty set at 3–15% of output. Both model agreements exclude foreign participation in projects in previously explored territories, but give investors a monopoly on oil-related activities in the contract area and the right to construct pipelines.

As and when commercial production from a field starts, both model agreements stipulate that the only tax that will apply to foreign investors is the 25% profit tax, and it will apply only after initial investments are recouped and then only on non-reinvested profits. Foreign investors in a JV will have to pay royalty and rent on the contractual area, but will be allowed to deduct these and other expenses from taxable profits. The model PSA promises compensation for new taxes and the model JV agreement has the same grandfathering clause as the law on foreign investment. Investors have to give preference to Turkmen suppliers, finance social projects and ensure the training of local personnel and transfer of advanced technology.

The model agreements have been criticized for imposing too narrow restrictions on investors' freedom of movement. An investor must present detailed annual work programmes and budgets to a project steering committee including representatives of the Ministry of Oil and Gas, and once the committee approves the programme/budget, the investor loses the flexibility to make even minor adjustments in expenditures during the year in question. Punishment for transgressions will be swift and severe – a 30-day delay in payments to the state, an 'unreasonable' suspension of operations or any other failure to fulfil contractual obligations may prompt the Ministry of Oil and Gas to terminate the agreement.

In March 1997 a new Law on Hydrocarbon Resources came into force. Companies have welcomed it as a step in the right direction. Drafted by ENEL but considerably revised by the State Investment Agency which found it too company-friendly, the law lays down rules for holding tenders, issuing licences and preparing contracts, and codifies tax exemptions that until now have been granted to oil companies on a case-by-case basis.

Changes in licensing procedures will make it more difficult for the government to suspend companies' right to export, as it did to Bridas and Larmag. The law acknowledges two contract types, JVs and PSAs, thereby accommodating the strong preference of companies for PSAs. Henceforth oil companies will pay only a profit tax, royalty and certain bonuses, and will not have to worry about rate increases and new taxes or levies; the law stipulates that a company's tax bill be held constant for the duration of its contract. More generally, the law promises to make life simpler for companies by replacing a system in which they have to deal with a number of state agencies with one in which they will receive all permits, approvals' authorizations and licences from a single agency called the Competent Authority. This body, which will be chaired by President Niyazov himself, will consult mainly with the State Agency for Foreign Investment, a body established in 1996. The Ministry of the Oil and Gas Industry and Mineral Resources seems to have been completely sidelined as concerns decisions on foreign investment.

Company lawyers, however, are reserving final judgment on the law until they have seen it practised. In particular, they are concerned about ambiguous formulations on procedures and obligations in the event of company–government disputes. Companies may take disputes to international arbitration, but it appears that the Turkmen government may well decide to ignore arbitrators' rulings; it has not signed either of the two conventions that bind local courts to enforce such rulings.

Gas production

Gas was discovered in Turkmenistan in 1951. Production peaked at almost 90 bcm in 1989, declined slowly in 1990 and 1991, dipped by 30% in 1992, recovered in 1993 but plunged to below 36 bcm a year in 1994–6. Output has fallen mainly because solvent demand has withered away. Turkmenistan has a swap arrangement with Russia whereby Turkmen gas is used in southern Russia while Siberian gas is sold to Ukraine and other FSU republics on Turkmenistan's account. Dramatic declines in GNP have led to declines in the energy needs of these republics, and, more important, disagreement on prices and mounting inter-republican energy debts have prompted cuts in energy deliveries. Turkmenistan has not been inclined to take a softer line than Russia on gas pricing and payment issues; on the contrary, Ashgabat started right after the break-up of the Union to charge what were considered to be world-level prices.

Another reason for the drop in Turkmenistan's gas exports – and a key reason for the fall in its hard-currency incomes – is a Russian decision made in late 1993 to terminate an arrangement whereby each year Turkmenistan had delivered a certain amount of gas to Russia and been credited for exports of a similar amount of Russian gas to Europe.

It is likely that not only Turkmenistan's actual gas output but also its immediately available gas production and export capacity has declined since 1991. Chronically short of funds and drained of know-how and technology, the gas industry has not been able to maintain fields and pipelines, much less to carry out exploration and develop new fields in accordance with long-term plans. Exactly how severely the republic's key gas fields and infrastructure have deteriorated is hard to say. That would become evident only if production suddenly ceased to be constrained from the demand side.

The jewel in the Turkmen gas crown is the giant Dauletabad-Donmez field near

13

Seraks on the border with Iran. Discovered in 1974, its reserves were initially put at 1,360 bcm. However, they are now thought to be almost three times bigger. In 1982 what was believed to be another giant field containing more than 2,000 bcm of gas was discovered 24 km south of Dauletabad-Donmez and named Sovietabad. Later, Soviet geologists realized that the two fields were in fact parts of the same structure. Dauletabad-Donmez – about 80% of whose recoverable reserves are still untapped – figures prominently in Turkmenistan's ambitions to export gas not only to Europe, Pakistan and India, but also to China and Japan.

The Soviet engineers charged with developing the field ran into numerous problems related to its very complex geological structure, high formation pressure and gas characterized by high contents of sulphur, CO_2 and wax. Drilling programmes fell behind schedule and delays in commissioning gas treatment plants also occurred. The northern end of the structure came on-stream only in 1983 and the southern end – i.e., the Sovietabad end – in 1984. Output quickly became significant, but has not increased at the envisaged pace. Since 1992 the Turkmen authorities may have had neither the incentives nor the funds to develop the field further.

Future production from Dauletabad is hard to forecast, depending as it will on market and geopolitical developments. However, the field is clearly an even bigger potential than actual engine for the Turkmen economy. As and when output can be increased to the level seen as possible in the light of estimated reserves – one source[6] estimates that it could yield 100–120 bcm a year – it could contribute significantly to the supply of several importing countries.

Other important Turkmen gas fields include Shatlyk (which once accounted for half of Turkmenistan's gas output and – although going into decline in 1983 – remains an important producer and a key pipeline junction), the Malay, Saman Tepe, Naip, Kirpichili and Achak fields in eastern Turkmenistan, and the Ekizak gas field and the Kotur Tepe and Korpedzhe oil and gas-condensate fields in the western part of the country. Construction of a gas processing plant with a capacity of 4 bcm a year to serve the Saman Tepe and nearby fields in the Amu Darya valley is on the government's list of priority projects.

In apparent defiance of the lack of solvent demand, President Niyazov ordered that gas production be boosted to 50–60 bcm in 1995, and issued a similar order for 1996. Predictably, those gestures had no impact on actual production. Initially, the output target for 1997 was a more modest 44 bcm, but a month or so into the year government spokesmen started talking about 53 bcm, referring to a Russian offer to reinstate a swap arrangement whereby Gazprom had credited Turkmenistan for a portion of Russian gas exports outside the FSU. The Turkmen authorities now see

[6] PetroStudies Co. (1995).

14

exports in 1997 amounting to 40 bcm, with 20 bcm going to Ukraine and the other 20 bcm to new FSU customers, such as Belarus, and to eastern Europe. However, Turkmen gas production during January–May was reported at no more than 11.3 bcm, down 37% on production during the same period in 1996, and the practical consequences of whatever has been agreed remain to be seen. During the summer, Turkmen–Russian relations apparently reached a low point, with President Niyazov complaining that Russia again offered access to pipelines only to other FSU republics. Russia has evident interests in Turkmenistan's political loyalty and petroleum reserves. On the other hand, its prime motivation for clamping down on Turkmenistan's access to the European gas market in the first place – Gazprom's need to secure as high a share as possible of this market for itself – remains in force.

Kazakstan

The Kazak oil and gas sector is characterized by significant and increasing private participation. Most known, attractive fields not already developed have been or are in the process of being awarded to JVs between Kazak and foreign firms. In 1996 such ventures accounted for about 50% of total Kazak gas production. Besides encouraging foreign investment in new or partially developed fields, the government has put out to tender a number of activities which only a couple of years ago seemed destined to remain with the state forever, such as managing the gas trunk pipeline system. This drive testifies to a conviction held by key Kazak policy-makers that economic reform along the lines recommended by the international financial institutions is unavoidable. It is also a pragmatic response to budgetary problems on the one hand and increasing dissatisfaction with state-owned oil and gas operators' results on the other.

In early 1997, prompted by low levels of efficiency and pockets of opposition to reform in the energy sector, President Nazarbayev ordered a major reorganization of the sector. Three ministries will be merged into one Ministry of Energy and Natural Resources: the Ministry of Oil and Gas, which concludes contracts with foreign companies and supervises operations along the oil and gas supply chains, in particular the operations of the national oil company Munaygaz and the national gas company Kazakgaz; the Ministry of Geology, which deals with mineral resource management and licensing; and the Ministry of Energy and Coal, which is in charge of the electricity and coal-mining industries. A separate Committee for Investment will be established to handle negotiations with foreign oil companies. Finally, a national oil company, Kazak Oil, is being set up to manage the government's oil and gas business interests.

In mid-1995 the Kazak government put the state's shares in the Aktyubinskneft and Yuzhneftegaz oil-producing companies and the Chimkent refinery out to international tender. At the same time a process of corporatizing other enterprises belong-

15

ing to Munaygaz and Kazakgaz took off. During 1996 restructuring and privatization of the oil and gas sector accelerated. The government decided to tender its portions of the gas transmission pipelines transporting Central Asian gas to Russia and Russian gas to Kazakstan and onward to other FSU republics and Europe. Investors were offered 15-year concessions. In return for management control and transit fees, they would have to maintain and, where necessary, rehabilitate the pipelines in addition to paying royalties and taxes. Several companies purchased bidding documents, presumably on the assumption that control over the pipelines across Kazak territory could be useful in negotiations with Russia for access to export markets. For some time Bridas of Argentina seemed the leading candidate, but eventually the Kazak government – reportedly dissatisfied with the Latin American company's investment proposal – awarded the contract to Tractebel of Belgium. Generally, the pace of the petroleum sector privatization process has slowed down in the wake of the restructuring of the sector, possibly owing to pressure from Kazak Oil.

Investment framework conditions

Through 1993 the Kazak government proceeded hesitantly with stabilization policies as well as with structural reforms. In 1994, however, President Nazarbayev – apparently realizing that past policies would deliver neither growth nor price stability, and under increasing pressure from the international financial institutions – ordered a series of stabilization and liberalization measures. The economy appears to have bottomed out in 1995 and preliminary figures indicate a growth of 1% in 1996. Inflation meanwhile has declined to between 30% and 40% a year. The government is trying to implement a fairly radical corporatization and privatization programme and a management contract scheme to foster the restructuring of large enterprises. The European Bank for Reconstruction and Development (EBRD) estimates that by early 1996 the so-called non-state sector of the economy, which includes companies with minority private shareholdings, accounted for more than 50% of GDP, while the share of the genuinely private sector was probably about 40%. However, privatization of non-energy enterprises is behind schedule, the management contract scheme has so far met with limited success, and even the energy-sector privatization programme – widely hailed for its boldness – has come under scrutiny. Observers are wondering why so few major international oil and gas companies are showing any interest, with the consequence that small, sometimes virtually unknown actors are picking up the assets, while at home those who are driving the process are being criticized for overextending themselves and selling off the family silver too cheaply.

Since late 1994 much new legislation of relevance to foreign investment in the oil and gas sector has been passed. President Nazarbayev dissolved parliament in March

1995 partly out of frustration with the slow pace at which draft laws made their way through the legislative branch of government. Throughout January 1996 he enjoyed the right to sign edicts with the force of law without having to account to parliamentarians, and he used the opportunity to the full. Although a new parliament was elected and convened by the end of January, edicts signed in late 1995 provide for a lasting increase in the powers of the president at the expense of the powers of parliament.

In December 1994, before the events that led up to its dissolution, parliament managed to pass a new law on foreign direct investment (FDI). It was generally welcomed as representing a significant step forward on its predecessor dating from 1990. The new law covers a broader array of activities than the old one, giving foreign investors the right to undertake any investment in any sort of property with the purpose of earning profits, and engage in any activity not prohibited by Kazak law. They may take a stake in privatized state concerns, but this right is qualified; there are provisions intended to support Kazak investors in the competition over state assets. Unlike its predecessor, the 1994 law explicitly guarantees foreign investors non-discriminatory treatment *vis-à-vis* other similarly situated foreign investors and *vis-à-vis* domestic investors. There are, however, qualifications to these guarantees too, and neither of them applies in privatization situations.

The law contains a stabilization clause protecting foreign investors from adverse changes in Kazak law for ten years from the date of the initial investment. Investments undertaken under longer-term contracts or licences are guaranteed legal stability for the duration of the contract or licence. The law explicitly prohibits nationalization or expropriation of foreign investments, but allows for expropriations 'in the national interest' provided that they follow the established legal procedure and are non-discriminatory. It sets forth detailed default procedures for resolving disputes. Unless they have established a different procedure, the parties to a dispute must first attempt to resolve it by negotiation, and then, if they fail, submit the dispute to an international dispute settlement body.

The law reins in the ability of the Cabinet of Ministers and other government agencies to conclude, approve and guarantee contracts with foreign investors, stipulating that only state entities that have been authorized by legislation or presidential decree to make promises to foreign investors in the name of the Republic of Kazakstan may pledge the assets of the state. Thus, foreign oil and gas companies are less likely to waste time and money talking to the wrong people in Kazakstan than, say, in Russia.

In April 1995 President Nazarbayev signed an edict amounting to a new tax code, reducing the number of applicable taxes from 45 to 19. The corporate enterprise profits tax rate was set at 30% for Kazak legal entities and, effectively, 40.5% for establishments operating in Kazakstan through branches. Depreciation rules were amended and simplified, loss-carry forward provisions were extended (though not as much as companies would have liked) and the rules on allowable expenses were liberalized. The code also established a regime for the taxation of the use of the 'subsurface' including oil and gas extraction, stipulating payments to the state budget in the form of bonuses, royalties and windfall profit taxes.

Most foreign investors have welcomed the new tax code although some of its provisions are less favourable than those they replace when applied to particular investment situations. Generally, foreign oil and gas companies have taken a different view, arguing that one key concept in the new code – that of uniform taxation across industries, implying a rescinding of benefits previously granted to investors in the oil and gas sector – places a near intolerable tax burden on them.

In June 1995 President Nazarbayev issued an edict amounting to a new petroleum law. Companies and observers had for some time urged political leaders to reform the country's laws on oil and gas activities, specifically to remove ambiguities and inconsistencies and adjust the regime in accordance with international norms. The new law went some way towards meeting foreign oil companies' concerns. In January 1996 the president issued another edict amounting to a new mining law. Sharing many provisions with the petroleum law, this law brought a higher degree of consistency to the legal framework for the development of subsurface minerals.

The mining law recognizes four types of contracts: PSAs, concession contracts, service contracts and joint operation contracts. Reflecting pressure from reformers, the new legislation contains a broad requirement for competitive bidding. However, there is a proviso permitting the government to conduct direct negotiations with investors. In the past, such negotiations have been the rule rather than the exception, with companies bypassing ongoing tenders on the basis of one-time cash bonus payments into Kazakstan's state budget. International financial institutions and others have criticized this practice for its lack of transparency.

Gas production

Kazakstan has never been a major gas producer, but output increased steadily from 2–3 bcm a year at the beginning of the 1970s to 6.85 bcm in 1991. The period 1992–6 saw production declining by a total of 40%, mainly because southern Russia, which traditionally takes a high share of Kazak gas, has recently been brimming with Russian gas. However, production reportedly recovered by 18% from the first quarter of 1996 to the same period of 1997.[7]

Kazaks pin their gas hopes mainly on Karachaganak, a huge gas-condensate

---

[7] Economist Intelligence Unit, *Country Report on Kazakstan*, 2nd quarter 1997.

field which could contain as much as 1,300 bcm of gas, 6.8 billion barrels of condensate and some crude oil. Located in the Uralsk region, it was discovered in 1979, partly developed by the Soviet gas industry and put on-stream in 1984. Output was projected to increase to 25 bcm a year of gas and 370,000 barrels a day (b/d) of liquids. Instead, production peaked in 1991 at 4 bcm, corresponding to about 60% of total Kazak gas production, and in 1996 the field yielded only 2 bcm, corresponding to 47% of the total.

There are several reasons for this disappointing performance. Russian needs for the field have declined. Since it was put on-stream, Karachaganak gas has been sent across the Kazak–Russian border to the Orenburg gas complex – a distance of only some 50 km (initially, Russian geologists thought that the Karachaganak and Orenburg fields were parts of the same structure) – for processing and distribution to regional users, while Karachaganak liquids have been sent via Orenburg to the Salavat and Ufa refineries in the Russian republic of Bashkortostan. In a situation characterized by oversupply, Gazprom understandably gives preference to its own gas. And the Karachaganak operators have no access to any other markets. The field is located so far away from Kazakstan's population and industrial centres that until now building pipelines to sell the gas domestically has been deemed too costly. Gazprom meanwhile, reluctant to create even more competition for itself, is denying Karachaganak gas access to its export pipelines.

Apart from these problems, Karachaganak has proved a difficult, costly and time-consuming field to develop. The Soviet engineers deployed to bring it on-stream ran into a series of problems related to the depth and pressure of the reservoir. By the time of the break-up of the FSU it was clear that developing the field further would be too big an undertaking for Kazakgas. In 1992 the government put it out to tender. Two Western companies – British Gas (BG) and Agip – were awarded the right to negotiate a field development plan and a PSA. They envisaged exporting both the gas and the liquids. Karachaganak gas did not and still does not meet export quality standards; high levels of sulphur characterize the output from the field, as from the Tengiz oilfield further south. This problem can be dealt with as and when opportunities for exports arise.

Negotiations dragged on, however, in part owing to disagreement between the Kazak authorities and the companies on how to dispose of the gas from the field, but mainly because of the refusal by Gazprom and Transneft to grant the Karachaganak operators any access whatsoever to their export pipelines.

To accommodate Russian interests, the Kazak government, BG and Agip agreed to invite Gazprom on board, and in December 1994 the Russian company became a partner. In early March 1995 an 'interim production-sharing principles agreement' was signed, giving British Gas and AGIP each a 42% stake and Gazprom 15% in the

'Karachaganak Operating Structure' (KOS).[8] The interim agreement, which would be in force for two to four years, provided for a restoration of gas and liquids production to their 1991 levels and securing the field. In the meantime the parties would work out final development, production-sharing and transportation agreements under a 40-year production licence.

Discussion within the KOS quickly ran into difficulties, however. Gazprom refused to contribute any money, claiming that it had already, between 1979 and 1991, sunk some 4.5 billion 1991 roubles (equivalent to US$90 million) into the project, and arguing that this investment not only should be counted as payment for its 15% stake, but warranted a higher stake. The Western partners did not accept Gazprom's reasoning. Consequently no progress was made on the issue of further access to Gazprom pipelines.

During 1996 a solution was worked out whereby Gazprom would sell all or part of its stake in KOS to LUKoil. The latter company has cash flow problems and struggles to finance its ventures outside Russia, but presumably its strategic partner Arco will foot the bill. LUKoil has no leverage on Gazprom and can hardly be of great help in securing access to Gazprom pipelines. It thus seems as if the project sponsors have come to consider exports of Karachaganak gas outside the FSU to be a fairly distant prospect. In the meantime they can reinject the gas or sell it domestically, and export liquids. Condensate and crude oil can be shipped via Russian pipelines to which LUKoil has access, or – in the future – via the pipeline to be built by the Caspian Pipeline Consortium. A project to build a southbound liquids line that will connect with the CPC line is under discussion.

The Kazak authorities have long tried to interest the Western KOS partners in allocating Karachaganak gas to Kazak consumers, namely in shipping it eastwards via a new pipeline to areas which today are without gas supply. The Western companies have never warmed to this project, which would generate only local currency (tenge), and possibly not even an abundance of that; inter-enterprise debts are a problem in Kazakstan as in the rest of the FSU. However, Tractebel, the Belgian company which in the spring of 1997 won a tender for a 15-year concession to manage Kazakstan's gas pipeline system, reportedly had to undertake to build a pipeline from Karachaganak to Akmola, the new capital. Such a line could at a later stage be extended to China, another plan long pursued by the Kazak leadership. The line to Akmola would have a capacity of 11–12 bcm a year and cost about $750 million. Evidently, if it is realized, analysts might have to revise their Kazak gas consumption forecasts upward and their gas export forecasts correspondingly downward.

---

[8] Since the foreign partners' combined stake in the field development project had itself been set at 15%, with the Kazak government (represented by Kazakgas) holding the remaining 85%, this split meant that British Gas and Agip were left with 6.375% each and Gazprom with a 2.25% interest in the field.

There is speculation that Gazprom's withdrawal from the project and the Western partners' pondering of solutions not involving Russian gas processing facilities and pipelines at all are moves in a positioning game rather than final statements. Gazprom needs Karachaganak gas for its Orenburg plant, and the Kazak government and the Western members of the contractor group (which now includes Texaco) need to be on speaking terms with Gazprom.

Meanwhile, not only is output from Karachaganak declining, but the field itself is deteriorating. The contractor group members are reluctant to commit large sums of money, not knowing when and under what circumstances they will be allowed to market output from the field. Consequently, investments are kept at minimum levels.[9]

Next to the Karachaganak operators, Uzenmunaygaz, which used to be part of the Munaygaz organization and operates fields on the Mangyshlak peninsula, is Kazakstan's biggest gas producer. In 1996 the unit produced about 1.7 bcm. Next on the list of operators are Aktobemunaygaz and Mangistaumunaygaz, two other Munaygaz group members operating in the Aktyubinsk area and on the Mangyshlak and Buzachi peninsulas respectively. Together they produce only about 0.3–0.4 bcm a year.

In the long term, a high share of Kazakstan's gas production could come from offshore fields. In late 1993 a group of Western oil companies signed an agreement with the government on funding a major 2D seismic study of the Kazak portion of the Caspian Sea in exchange for exclusive rights to negotiate PSAs for selected blocks of the area. The study was to be carried out by Kazakstancaspishelf (KCS), a state-owned company established to represent the government in all offshore projects with personnel seconded from the consortium partners. The survey – the biggest of its kind ever carried out – was completed ahead of schedule in 1996 at a cost of more than $200 million. Altogether 26,500 line-km of seismic were shot. An area of about 100,000 square kilometres, i.e., about one-quarter of the total area of the Caspian Sea, was covered. On the basis of preliminary results of the survey, consortium members put potential resources in the area at 3.5 billion tons of oil and 2 trillion cubic metres of gas. Currently the talk is about oil, which is easier to market; thus, Kazakstancaspishelf and a US engineering company have completed an infrastructure feasibility study premised on a rise in offshore oil production from an initial 100,000 b/d by 2004 to 1.2 million b/d by 2013. Later, however, as and when political and infrastructural conditions for their development fall into place, the gas under the Caspian seabed could become a very valuable resource.

---

[9] BG and AGIP reportedly plan to invest only $65 million in Karachaganak during 1997, i.e. one-third less than they invested during 1996. The Kazak partner in the project has reportedly threatened to shut the field down owing to non-payment for condensate deliveries to the Ufa and Salavat refineries.

Uzbekistan

Although Uzbekistan is currently the leading gas producer in the Caspian area, energy business journals carry few stories about Uzbek gas affairs compared to their coverage of Turkmen gas, Kazak oil and gas and Azeri oil dealings. There are two reasons for this apparent dearth of news from Uzbekistan. In the first place, the country produces gas mainly for its own consumption. The export dimension is almost absent, and the tugs-of-war between proponents of alternative export routes are correspondingly low key. Secondly, and closely related to the inward orientation of the Uzbek gas industry, foreign companies are almost absent from the scene. Neither of these factors keeping Uzbekistan away from the spotlight may last forever, however. The country could well become a regionally important if not world-class gas exporter, and the Karimov government is taking steps to attract foreign companies.

In May 1992 a national Uzbek oil and gas company was established by merging the existing enterprises in charge of upstream activities, oil refining and product distribution, gas transmission and distribution and petroleum facility construction. More recently, this company, Uzbekneftegas, also took over also the enterprises responsible for petroleum exploration which until then had reported to the Uzbek Committee on Geology. The president of Uzbekneftegaz is also deputy prime minister.

As noted, foreign oil and gas companies have not contributed much to the development of Uzbekistan's petroleum resources. By early 1997 only one such company, the Malaysia-based Probady, held E&P rights and was carrying out field development work. LUKoil had formed a JV with Uzbekneftegas to develop some fields, and Enron, Texaco, Pertamina and Unocal had signed letters of intent with the Uzbek company, but only Enron was actually negotiating for E&P rights.

Uzbekistan's relatively autarchic policy on oil and gas development is, however, coming to an end. In 1996 the government made a resolute attempt to broaden its contacts with Western, especially US, firms. A delegation headed by President Karimov toured Houston and Washington DC with a presentation of nine blocks whose proven oil, condensate and gas reserves are estimated at 351 million tonnes, 11 million tonnes and 143 bcm respectively and whose probable reserves are much bigger. In 1995 foreign energy related investment in Uzbekistan came to $365 million, and the government hopes to have attracted more than $1 billion a year by 1998.

Investment framework conditions

The Uzbek economy has contracted little by FSU standards, partly because the Uzbek authorities have proceeded carefully with economic reform; prices have been freed at a measured pace with the government backtracking on liberalization moves when the results have seemed too destabilizing, and by the end of 1993 very little genuine privatization and almost no restructuring had taken place.

A plan for privatizing medium and large-scale enterprises was launched in early 1994, however, and a mass privatization scheme involving vouchers and investment funds is under preparation. By late 1996 the share of the non-state sector in GDP was estimated at 67%. The share of the private sector is probably closer to 40%. The state will retain, at least for the time being, controlling interests in strategic industries such as oil and gas, electricity and gold mining.

In September 1995 the Uzbek parliament adopted a resolution removing oil and gas companies from the list of enterprises reserved for full state control. Reportedly the IMF had insisted on some measure of privatization of the petroleum industry as a condition for granting further loans. By the end of 1995 some 50–60 oil and gas enterprises units had been privatized, and the government had signalled a willingness to consider private bids even for pipelines.

It remains to be seen whether the Uzbek authorities, by taking a gradualist approach to reform, have managed to stave off permanently the economic turbulence characterizing other FSU republics or whether they will have to pay a price in the form of lower growth rates in the years ahead. Until 1996 indications were positive: reforms were finally being implemented but without causing as much dislocation as similar steps had done elsewhere in the FSU; Uzbekistan enjoyed the support of the IMF, the World Bank and the EBRD; and foreign investors were showing considerable interest. However, further delays of a mass privatization programme and a tightening of import controls and restrictions on currency convertibility in the context of sluggish economic growth have recently brought grist to the mills of the sceptics.

The main law governing FDI, 'On foreign investment and guarantees for the activity of foreign investors', was adopted in May 1994. The law stipulates that foreign investors shall be treated no less favourably than national ones and that foreign investments cannot be expropriated or nationalized except in the case of natural disasters, accidents or epidemics. However, compensation mechanisms have not been defined. A grandfathering clause provides that law amendments leading to a worsening of conditions for an investor shall not apply for up to ten years from the date of registration of the investment. Disputes between foreign investors and state bodies will be settled in national courts. If both parties agree, however, disputes can be settled by courts of arbitration, including foreign courts.

The law stipulates that foreign investors can remit abroad profits and other funds without any limitation, have accounts in any currency with local banks, and use their national currency accounts to buy foreign currency. Currency proceeds – after taxes and deductions – from exports of own production can be retained. However, foreign investors operating under the foreign investment law are generally expected to run foreign currency neutral operations and not to require access to Uzbekistan's limited foreign currency reserves. There are no guarantees that the currency markets at any time will have the necessary foreign currency to sell, and at times such shortages have been a problem.

Western observers consider Uzbekistan's foreign investment legislation to be reasonably investor-friendly, but add that other pieces of legislation have apparently been drafted without the interests of foreign investors in mind. For example, the enterprise registration procedure is bureaucratic and time-consuming, and currency regulations can make banking procedures equally cumbersome. Moreover, in some regions foreign investors face heavy local government interference.

The tax system continues to reflect pre-independence relationships and needs and is some way from meeting Western equity, neutrality and simplicity standards. However, improvements have been enacted and a better system appears to be on the horizon. The general profit tax rate is 37%, while JVs with more than 30% foreign participation and wholly-owned foreign enterprises pay 25%. If more than 30% of an enterprise's production is exported, its profits tax rate is reduced by half. JVs fulfilling the 30% foreign participation requirement are offered five-year tax holidays. All enterprises including foreign ones are liable to VAT, which at present is 18%. Foreign investors – dependent upon sector – may also face subsurface tax, excise tax, property tax, land tax and contributions to various state funds.

With respect to oil and gas legislation, a Law on Concessions was adopted in August 1995 with the intention of regulating the relationship between the state and foreign investors in the natural resources sector. Western observers have noted many omissions and contradictions in the law. For instance, it does not specify which state body or bodies have the authority to enter into concession agreements, no registration procedure has been established, fee procedures and amounts remain to be decided, and taxation rules remain obscure.

Gas production

Uzbekistan has been an oil and gas producer for more than 100 years, but field development on a large scale commenced only in the 1950s. Production increased dramatically when the Gazli field located about 100 km northwest of Bukhara was brought on-stream. At its peak Gazli yielded well over 20 bcm a year. It went into decline in the mid-1970s, but a group of smaller fields around Mubarek were commissioned in time to keep total production from dropping noticeably, and in 1980 another giant field, Shurtan, located 150 km northeast of Bukhara, was put on-stream. Since 1987 Shurtan has yielded as much gas per year as Gazli did at its peak. It could probably sustain an output of 30 bcm a year.

Whereas Gazli gas is free of sulphur dioxide, the other fields yield mostly sour gas, which must be treated either at the Shurtan gas chemical complex, or at the Mubarek gas processing and sulphur recovery complex, which has 15 production units and a total nameplate capacity of 30 bcm a year.

The post-independence years have seen steady growth in Uzbekistan's oil and gas production, for three main reasons: the bulk of output is consumed domestically; the Uzbek economy has contracted less than the average for the former Soviet republics, resulting in relatively minor declines in domestic oil and gas use; and – on the supply side – there has been a timely phasing in of new fields as production from old ones has declined.

In the first six months of 1997 Uzbekistan produced 3.861 mt of oil and condensate (a 1% increase on the same period of 1996) and 25.6 bcm of natural gas (1.5% increase).[10]

Other Central Asia

Kyrgyzstan's and Tajikistan's aggregate gas production in 1996 amounted to a modest 60 million cubic metres. In recent years both countries have experienced strong declines in oil and gas investment and production, as a result of economic crisis and – in the case of Tajikistan – civil war.

Kyrgyzstan's gas production declined from more than 100 million cubic metres a year in the late 1980s to about 30 mcm in 1996. Output now covers only about 5% of the electricity industry's and residential consumers' needs. Kyrgyzneft, the state enterprise responsible for oil and gas E&P, has almost no money for development drilling, let alone for exploration.

Gas transmission and distribution was the responsibility of Kyrgyzgaz until early 1997 when that enterprise and two others, Chugazmunaizat (oil and gas trading and financing) and Kyrgyzmunaizat (oil trade and refining) were merged into a new state oil and gas trading company which will operate under the name of Kyrgyzmunaizat. One foreign company, Kyrgoil Corporation, registered in Canada, holds E&P rights in Kyrgyzstan. A 50–50 Kyrgoil-Kyrgyzneft JV has exclusive rights to work over the country's 630 oil and gas wells, half of which are inactive. The Kyrgyz authorities hope, however, to attract more foreign investment in the petroleum sector. In 1994 they invited companies to tender for E&P rights in seven blocks in six different basins, but failed to attract any interest. During the autumn of 1996 they again announced, on considerably softened terms, a tender for the same blocks, two of which are assumed to hold a total of 25 bcm of gas in addition to oil. It remains to be seen whether companies will find the Kyrgyz market – where all oil and gas

[10] Interfax Petroleum Report, vol. VI, issue 34, 22–29 August 1997.

25

would have to be sold – sufficiently interesting, and the stability and convertibility of the Kyrgyz currency, the som, sufficiently assured, to warrant sizeable longer-term commitments.

Tajikistan's gas production in 1985 exceeded 300 million cubic metres, but already by the time of the break-up of the FSU output had declined to about 100 million cubic metres a year, and by 1996 it had fallen by another two-thirds. Tajikgeologiya and Tajikneft, the state enterprises in charge of exploratory drilling and oil and gas production respectively, are suffering to an even higher degree than their counterparts in the other smaller Central Asian and Caucasian republics from a scarcity of funds and inputs of all kinds. The Tajik media reported in the spring of 1997 that industrial gas users in Dushanbe had run up debts to the tune of 900 million Tajik roubles with the local distributor, while household consumers owed 870 million roubles; the Dushanbe administration contemplated rationing gas supplies to selected customers to drive home the message that gas bills have to be paid.

There are no foreign rightholders in war-ravaged Tajikistan's petroleum industry, and apparently no plans to organize tenders of any kind.

Located outside or on the margins of the major oil and gas basins in the region, and with small proven and probable gas reserves, Kyrgyzstan and Tajikistan are probably doomed to remain marginal petroleum producers. Political stabilization, reform policies and specific measures to attract foreign oil and gas companies could lift output rates, but on present indications not very much. However, even modest increases would matter to the countries themselves, reducing their vulnerability to cuts in imported fuel supplies and improving their trade balances.

Azerbaijan

Although Azerbaijan is considered a potential world-class oil producer and exporter, the republic is not widely expected to become a gas heavyweight. Most observers seem to consider self-sufficiency in gas rather than a position as a major exporter to be a reasonable target. Some of the offshore fields slated for development are thought to contain significant amounts of gas, but many producing fields are in steep decline, so only fairly modest net output additions are expected as the new fields come on-stream. Many Azeris and some observers are challenging this view, however, in the belief that the Azeri sector of the Caspian Sea holds much more gas than is normally assumed, and also in view of the potential in refurbishing old fields. They see the export pipeline situation fairly quickly becoming the binding constraint on production, and are already looking at alternative pipeline routes and export marketing possibilities.

Azerbaijan does not have a fuel and energy ministry or a similar body charged with drawing up policy for the entire energy sector. According to the prime minister, such a ministry will be established, but currently a small number of state companies formulate and implement policy at sub-sector level. The most important of these is Socar, the state oil company in charge of upstream operations including gas field development and gas production, while Azerigas handles gas imports, transmission, storage and distribution and gas pipeline construction.

Socar, an organization with some 80,000 staff and a byzantine internal structure, enjoys a high degree of autonomy in deciding on petroleum industry ends and means. It is not only developing and operating fields on its own account and representing the government in projects with foreign participation, but is also a key force in shaping these projects. Socar, not the Ministry of Foreign Economic Relations or some other ministry, negotiates PSAs with foreign companies, and prepares tenders, evaluates bids, selects winners and negotiates contracts with equipment supply and service companies. The Ministry of Foreign Economic Relations is called upon only at the end of negotiations to register contracts.

Socar has so far negotiated five major agreements with foreign company consortia, for the Guneshli/Chirag/Azeri fields and the Shah Deniz, Karabakh, Dan Ulduzu/Ashrafi and Lenkoran/Talish Deniz prospects. As the Azeri company has gained negotiating experience, terms have become tougher; for instance, whereas Socar has a stake of only 10% in the first of these projects, it holds 25% in the fifth and latest one.

Azerigas, with about 16,000 staff, has a more limited mandate: to buy gas from Socar and foreign suppliers and distribute it through regional transmission and distribution entities to over one million consumers including power plants, industry, communal service institutions and households.

The lack of a body such as a Ministry of Energy to direct and coordinate sub-sector activities has led to policy inconsistencies and a waste of resources. Most Western observers are urging the Azeri authorities to take the need for overall energy policy-making more seriously. At sub-sector level, both Socar and Azerigas, created in 1992 on the basis of numbers of existing state enterprises and other organizations, are regarded as seriously overstaffed and generally ineffective. The Azerigas management has proposed to turn the company into a state-owned joint stock company, and prepared a draft charter for government review. Such a step could pave the way for improvements in accounting practices and start a process of alerting company executives to the requirements of the market – though central and eastern Europe and the FSU have seen many corporatizations of enterprises that have had little or no effect on managers' outlook and behaviour and left the enterprise unprepared for privatization.

Gas production

Until the mid-1950s gas production was limited to associated production from onshore oilfields. In 1955, however, a large dry gas field – Karadag – was discovered some 40 km southeast of Baku, and the following years saw the discovery of several offshore gas fields such as Yuzhnaya, Bakhar and Bulla. Since then, gas production has primarily been offshore. Output increased from 9.9 bcm in 1975 to about 14 bcm a year in the mid-1980s. The late 1980s and early 1990s saw steep declines in production; in 1996 output amounted to only 6.3 bcm. The first quarter of 1997 brought no recovery, although the pace of decline slowed down.

Azerbaijan's oil and gas industry has been severely hit by regional and domestic political turmoil on top of the problems that have affected all the former Soviet republics, i.e., those related to the transition from central planning to market economic arrangements and to the breakdown in interrepublican trade. Gas production has declined also because there are few facilities for collecting associated gas produced offshore, meaning that a high proportion of gas produced at Guneshli and the second biggest offshore field, Neft Dashlary, is vented.[11] Of the remaining gas, Socar uses about 1 bcm a year in its own operations and delivers the rest either to the Karadag gas processing plant or directly into the Azerigas network.

Caught between declines in production and sales, non-payment for deliveries,[12] government claims on the money that is collected and limited opportunities to reorganize, shed staff and cut costs, Socar is chronically short of funds. The company's capacity to implement exploration programmes declined towards zero between 1992 and 1995 – in 1995 it drilled only about 2,000 m of exploratory and appraisal wells, implying a plan fulfilment ratio of 6%. The following year, however, saw a modest recovery.

As noted, the Azeri authorities pin their hopes for an upswing in gas production mainly on the big offshore fields that are being or will be developed by consortia of foreign companies. The Azeri and Chirag fields contain an estimated 170 bcm of gas in addition to oil and condensate; the Shah Deniz prospect – where drilling has not yet started and where the level of reserves is correspondingly uncertain – is thought to hold some 400–500 bcm; the Tagiev structure south of the Oil Rocks field could also contain around 400 bcm, and reserves in the Bakhar and Bakhar-2 areas southeast of Baku are estimated at about 100 bcm and 200 bcm respectively. The Dan Ulduzu/Ashrafi structures could contain 30–50 bcm.

In 1980 Azerbaijan was a net gas exporter to the tune of 20% of output; in 1990

---

[11] The commissioning of the Neft Dashlary gas plant led to a 4.2% increase in gas production from 1994 to 1995.
[12] By late 1996 Socar was reportedly owed some $140 million by the Ministry of Defence, the Ministry of Agriculture and Azerenergo, and another $360 million from other customers.

28

it had to import some 8.4 bcm to cover about 45% of domestic needs. Between 1991 and 1995 the country received an estimated 27 bcm, mainly from Turkmenistan. In the autumn of 1992 and again in the spring of 1994 Turkmenistan cut supplies as a response to mounting payment arrears. Lacking both hard currency and goods to pledge under barter arrangements, and probably encouraged by the outlook for increased indigenous gas production, the government decided that in 1995 it would not incur more gas debts, and instructed Azerigas to halt gas imports. Since then most of the country has been without gas – its 1996 output was directed mainly to Baku and Sumgait on the north side of the Apsheron peninsula where a high share of Azerbaijan's energy-intensive industry is located. Socar has been instructed to increase indigenous production as quickly as possible, but apparently no one has seen a concrete plan for speeding up developments.

Other Caucasus

Although Georgia produces some oil, neither it nor Armenia is a gas producer. The two countries are located outside or on the margins of the major oil and gas basins in the area, and seem to have miniscule gas reserves. Both of them are trying to attract foreign oil and gas companies, and if the geopolitics of the region stabilize and investors are offered attractive terms, they will no doubt see some exploration and development. However, there are no indications at present that either of them faces a major change in gas fortunes; self-sufficiency remains a distant dream.

Armenia's national gas company, Armtransgaz, is exceptionally short of funds and the government strives to attract foreign investment in the fuel sector. However, to date only one JV has been established. This venture, the American–Armenian Exploration Company, involving US-based Rand-Paulson, is to carry out seismic studies in two blocks in western Armenia, possibly do some exploration drilling and eventually produce petroleum under a PSA. Although Armenia has seen quite a bit of exploration – between 1947 and 1990 Soviet geologists shot a total of 3,250 line-km of seismic and drilled more than 200 exploratory wells – many wells did not reach planned depths.

Georgia also has a national petroleum industry. In late 1995 most state entities comprising the energy sector were consolidated into a single state enterprise, Sakenergo. In addition the Georgian International Oil Corporation (GIOC) was established to promote the building of a pipeline for Azeri oil across Georgia, but looking at upstream projects as well, and there are a few JVs between the Georgian state and foreign companies. The recent changes for the better in Georgia's fragile political and economic situation – and of course the AIOC decision to export some early oil via Georgia – have led to an upswing in foreign interest in the republic's energy resources. A few foreign companies, e.g. the UK-based JKX Oil and Gas (which reportedly is to be taken over by Ramco) and the Swiss-based National Petroleum, have signed PSAs, while several others have signed E&P protocol agreements.

Gas production is negligible: whereas the target for 1996 was 177 mcm, actual output amounted to 3.3 mcm. Reportedly, the main problem was a lack of equipment to harness gas produced together with oil. Thus, installing such equipment would raise gas production quickly and considerably in relative terms. Looking further ahead, however, the chances of making significant gas discoveries are seen as slimmer than those of finding more oil. The only non-associated gas activity reported is the development of two small fields near Tbilisi to meet local industry demand.

Table 2: Gas production, 1991–6 (bcm)

	1991	1992	1993	1994	1995	1996
Armenia	0.00	0.00	0.00	0.00	0.00	0.00
Azerbaijan	8.62	7.87	6.78	6.38	6.64	6.30
Georgia	0.05	0.04	0.02	0.02	0.01	0.00
Kazakstan	6.85	6.20	5.40	4.50	4.80	4.24
Kyrgyzstan	0.08	0.07	0.04	0.04	0.04	0.03
Tajikistan	0.09	0.06	0.04	0.03	0.04	0.03
Turkmenistan	79.56	55.70	65.20	35.80	35.60	35.36
Uzbekistan	41.88	42.60	42.00	47.20	46.60	48.10
Total	137.13	112.54	119.48	93.97	93.73	94.06

Sources: Petroconsultants; PlanEcon Inc.

Gas trade

In 1995 Turkmenistan, Kazakstan and Uzbekistan exported an estimated 31.8 bcm of gas. Deliveries to other Caspian countries accounted for about 50% of the total and deliveries to FSU republics outside the Caspian area for the rest. Kazakstan exported gas only to Russia, owing to the location of Kazak gas resources. Uzbekistan supplied only its Central Asian neighbours. Turkmenistan delivered gas to Ukraine, Russia and all other republics in the Caspian area except Uzbekistan.

Intraregional gas trade is characterized by payment problems and subsequent delivery cuts as are Turkmenistan's gas exports outside the Caspian area. As noted, the Azeri government has responded to Turkmenistan's post-independence gas pricing policy and arm-twisting for payment by deciding to do without Turkmen gas. The other south Caucasian governments have not felt able to adopt similar positions. By 1996 Georgia had reportedly run up gas depts to Turkmenistan to the tune of US$ 400 million. During the winter of 1995–6 Tbilisi received Turkmen gas on a cash-only basis with the result that imports dropped to one-sixth of their 1988 level. Armenian debts were smaller but significant compared to the size – after years of contraction – of the Armenian economy. Uzbekistan has used the weapon of delivery cut-off against Kazakstan, Kyrgyztan and Tajikistan.

Apart from payment problems, local political conflicts have interfered with deliveries. Georgia's and Armenia's supplies have frequently been interrupted as a consequence of sabotage on the North Ossetian segment of a key pipeline. There has also been sabotage on the Georgian segment of the line; between January 1994 and May 1995 it was reportedly damaged 36 times in the Marneuli and Bolnisi region alone. Armenia, being at the end of the line, is most vulnerable to sabotage. Armenians have complained about Georgians responding to supply shortfalls by siphoning off gas in transit to Armenia.

Existing gas transmission pipelines

The eight Central Asian and Caucasian republics have a total of about 37,000 km of gas transmission pipelines amounting to 17–18% of the total gas transmission pipeline grid of the FSU. There is a reasonably high degree of consistency in reporting on pipeline lengths and dimensions, but much variation across sources with respect to capacity estimates. Apparently, some sources quote design capacities while others try to adjust for wear and tear, poor maintenance and corrosion (which is extreme in parts of the Caspian area partly because of high salt contents in the soil). Unfortunately, sources are not always explicit about what they are referring to.

Located in the middle of Central Asia, and currently the area's biggest gas producer, Uzbekistan is the country of origin or serves as transit country for all intraregional gas flows, and also for Turkmenistan's gas exports outside the region. Thus it makes sense to begin an overview of the gas transmission pipeline network in the Caspian area with some comments on the main pipeline corridors and pipelines on Uzbek territory.

One pipeline system with lines varying in size from 1,020 to 520 mm runs eastward from Gazli and the fields around Bukhara via Samarkand to the Fergana valley in the far east of Uzbekistan, transiting northwestern Tajikistan on the way. Another system runs northeastward from those same fields via Tashkent, Chimkent and Dzhambul in Kazakstan, and Bishkek in Kyrgyzstan to Almaty in Kazakstan. Some sections of this system are reported to have throughput capacities of up to 26 bcm a year, but because of bottlenecks it can deliver significantly less to Almaty, possibly only about 3 bcm a year. As deliveries of Uzbek gas to Kazakstan in 1995 are estimated to have been almost 3 bcm, the need to upgrade this system could be urgent.

A third system of pipelines runs northwestward from the Bukhara area along the Uzbek bank of the Amu Darya river to Kungrad, an Uzbek compressor station south of the Aral Sea, and onward via western Uzbekistan and western Kazakstan all the way to Alexandrov Gay in Russia. At Khiva in Uzbekistan – about halfway between Gazli and Kungrad – this system receives gas via a 1,440 mm pipeline from Dauletabad and other fields in eastern Turkmenistan. Thus, the route onward to Alexandrov Gay is the main export route for Central Asian gas. At Kungrad two 1,020 mm lines branch off and run straight north along the Aral Sea, across Kazakstan and into the Volga Ural area in Russia to Chelyabinsk. Gas from the Aktyubinsk area in Kazakstan is fed into these lines via a spur. They can at present deliver about 3.2 bcm a year to Chelyabinsk.

Further northwest, at Beyneau in Kazakstan, the lines continuing towards Alexandrov Gay receive some of the gas produced in western Turkmenistan via a 1,220 mm pipeline starting almost at the Turkmen–Iranian border, providing an outlet for the fields scattered along the Caspian coast between Okarem and Nebit Dag, continuing via the narrow strip of land separating the Kara-Bogaz Gol from the Caspian Sea to Kazakstan and turning northeastward to pass the Uzen field before making the final 250 km or so to Beyneau. As indicated, this line serves consumers in western Turkmenistan and Kazakstan as well as export purposes. In recent years the share of output left for exports has declined in step with gas production in western Turkmenistan. Consequently, the Okarem–Beyneau pipeline, in particular its northernmost segment, is severely underutilized.

Northwest of Beyneau the system continuing towards Alexandrov Gay consists of up to five pipeline strings plus numerous additional loops. At Makat, some 150 km from Atyrau on the Kazak Caspian Sea coast, a 1020mm line branches off this system, heads southwestward to Atyrau and continues along the north coast of the Caspian Sea and via Astrakhan, Kalmykia and Dagestan in Russia to link up with the north Caucasian pipeline network. It is unclear whether this line is fully operable and whether it has served to move Turkmen gas to the south Caucasian republics or Russian gas from Astrakhan either via Makat to Alexandrov Gay or towards the Caucasus. From Alexandrov Gay some central Asian gas is directed eastward on the Soyuz export pipeline system, while the rest continues northward to Saratov and Moscow.

The pipelines from Gazli to Makat have a design capacity of 63 bcm a year while that of the system onward to Alexandrov Gay is 35 bcm a year and that of the line between Makat and the Caucasian republics is 28 bcm a year. The Soyuz export pipeline originating at the Russian Orenburg field across the border from the Kazak Karachaganak field and transiting northwestern Kazakstan has a design capacity of about 75 bcm a year. In 1997 Turkmenistan aims at exporting a total of 40 bcm of gas to Ukraine and central and eastern Europe and perhaps 2–3 bcm to Georgia and Armenia. Uzbekistan has agreed to supply another 6–10 bcm to Ukraine. All this gas has to be delivered physically to Russia, if not all the way to Ukraine and Europe, so it appears that Central Asian gas exports this year could correspond to 70–80% of total export pipeline design capacity with only 15–20 bcm of capacity left unused.[13]

In fact, exports could hit the pipeline capacity ceiling very soon as by and large actual capacities are significantly below design capacities. The trunk pipelines crossing Uzbek, Turkmen and Kazak territory are known to be in a precarious state. Since the break-up of the Soviet Union, the cessation of central funding of the republics' oil and gas industries and the emigration of Russian pipeline crews from Central Asia, there has been precious little maintenance. Long stretches are badly corroded and might crack if operated at their design pressure of 75 bars. In recent years they have been used at less than half their design capacities, and still there has been a string of minor and some major accidents. If utilization starts increasing, technical transit breakdowns could quickly become a major problem. Turkmenrosgaz was established on the premise that it would invest $300 million a year initially in the renovation of Turkmen pipelines and compressor stations. The Kazak government is privatizing the management of its gas transmission pipelines mainly to mobilize private capital for pipeline rehabilitation and maintenance.

Central Asian gas exports via Russia to Ukraine and Europe may also be constrained by the capacity of Gazprom's export pipelines. According to the study referred to above,[14] the aggregate capacity of pipelines moving gas into Ukraine is some 204 bcm, the capacity of pipelines continuing to central and western Europe 103 bcm and that of lines continuing to southeastern Europe 29 bcm. By 1995, all of these systems had spare capacity. But given Gazprom's export targets, envisaged deliveries will exceed pipeline capacities even by the turn of the century, and by 2010 the lines into and out of Ukraine could be inadequate to the tune of about 40 bcm a year. This suggests that, if the upgrading of Russian and Ukrainian pipelines and/or the development of a new export route via Belarus and Poland do not proceed apace, the Caspian republics can forget about exporting gas outside the FSU via Russia.

---

[13] There are higher export pipeline capacity estimates than those quoted above. Dr Michael Korchemkin, in a study quoted in *European Gas Markets*, 24 April 1997, puts the capacity of the Kungrad-Chelyabinsk pipeline at 28 bcm a year. *Russian Petroleum Investor*, in its December 1996–January 1997 edition, puts the capacity of the line to the Volga Ural area at 14 bcm and that of the Makat–North Caucasus line at 25.5 bcm a year. Both sources arrive at a total capacity of 110–20 bcm for existing pipelines leading out of Central Asia, indicating that exports could be increased quite a bit on the basis of existing infrastructure. However, one would have to assume the existence of pipelines with spare capacity to carry the gas onwards to solvent markets, as well as access to these pipelines, to draw the conclusion that the Central Asian states do not face infrastructural constraints on their gas exports.

[14] Korchemkin, op. cit. (note 13).

The south Caucasian republics import Russian gas via pipelines running from Yelets southward to Rostov-on-Don. From there, one line runs southeastward through Krasnodar, Stavropol and North Ossetia, turns southward at Mozdok, crosses the Caucasus Mountains, hits Tbilisi in Georgia and continues to Yerevan in Armenia. Another line continues southeastward from Mozdok to Makhachkala on the west coast of the Caspian Sea, and proceeds down the Caspian Sea coast to Baku. There is also one line running from Tuapse on the east coast of the Black Sea down the coast to Sukhumi in Abkhazia, Georgia, and onwards to Tbilisi.

Azeri gas is distributed mainly by means of a pipeline system originating at the offshore Oil Rocks field and running to Tbilisi via Baku and Kazi Mahomed, a pipeline junction southwest of Baku. Various short pipelines link Azerbaijan's other gas-producing fields with this system. The Azeris stopped using it for exporting gas to Georgia several years ago, both because segments of it are located almost on the Azerbaijani–Armenian border and because Azerbaijan no longer had gas available for exports. Branch lines bring gas to Azeri consumers north and south of the main corridor. The system is old, with some segments dating from the 1920s, and so are the compressor stations on it. As unprocessed gas containing water and heavier hydrocarbons makes up more than half of the gas delivered to Azerigas, pipeline corrosion is a big problem, and after years of inadequate maintenance the reliability of the system has gone from bad to worse. System losses including unmetered and unbilled consumption and leakages are thought to be around 15% of gas input. Around 1970 an import pipeline was built from Astara on the Iranian–Azeri border to Kazi Mahomed as an extension of the Iranian IGAT-1 line. A few years later a second string was built from Astara to Kazi Mahomed and onward to Kazakh. Imports reached about 9 bcm a year in the late 1970s. The gas was mainly transited to Armenia and Georgia. However, following the Iranian revolution the use of the line dwindled to zero.

Armenia receives gas from the Tbilisi–Baku system. One import pipeline branches off the Georgian part of the system a few kilometres northwest of the Georgian–Azeri border. Another originates at Kazakh in western Azerbaijan. These lines are linked to each other through a pipeline grid covering central and northern Armenia. A third line, unconnected to the others, runs southward from a point on the Tbilisi–Baku system west of Yevlakh in central Azerbaijan via Armenia to Nakhichevan. The pipelines entering Armenia from Azerbaijan were put out of operation at the outset of the Armenian–Azeri war at the end of the 1980s, leaving Armenia with one gas lifeline – the one coming from Georgia. Deliveries via this line have frequently been interrupted; gas lines are easy and popular terrorist targets. Some 70% of the Armenian population are within reach of the transmission pipeline network which consists of lines ranging in size from 720 to 1,020 mm and which – if fully operational – could carry about 5 bcm of gas a year to Armenia.

34

With improvements in the supply situations on the horizon (see section on new pipelines), the Armenian pipeline system is slated for rehabilitation. A recent EU-funded study concluded that a total refurbishment of the gas industry would cost $800 million. Investments on this scale are not on the short-term agenda. But a project to restart gas supplies to areas near the main transmission line in northern Armenia, and another project to install thousands of gas meters in homes and small businesses, are being implemented.

Table 3: Gas transmission pipelines in Central Asia and the Caucasus, 1992 (km)

	1,440 mm	1,220 mm	1,020 mm	Smaller	Total
Kazakstan	1,737	3,327	3,065	2,373	10,501
Kyrgyzstan	0	0	65	516	581
Tajikistan	0	0	74	790	864
Turkmenistan	1,879	906	2,293	2,259	7,337
Uzbekistan	564	1,930	4,029	4,063	10,586
Armenia	0	56	161	1,602	1,819
Azerbaijan	0	747	742	1,948	3,437
Georgia	0	84	89	1,741	1,914
Total	4,180	7,050	10,518	15,291	37,039

Source: PetroStudies Co.

Gas production forecasts

Oil and gas market analysts have become better at forecasting energy and individual fuel demand, but have by and large failed at developing tools to predict supply. Mainly because of a tendency to underestimate oil production, supply/demand model-based oil price projections have fallen into disgrace. Better exploration methods and tools, horizontal drilling, cost-cutting offshore related to the use of unmanned subsea production devices and the opening up of new countries and regions for Western oil companies, E&P are some of the factors that have confounded analysts, and could continue to do so.

With gas production forecasting there is an additional problem: in the absence, outside the United States, of spot markets, fields are seldom developed unless and until there are assured markets for the gas. Consequently, one has to make assumptions on individual market developments and individual buyers' and competitors' strategies in addition to prices, reserves and costs.

In some countries and regions, unsettled political, legal and other institutional frameworks affect investment and consequently future output; the FSU is a prominent

35

example. Finally, projecting Caspian area gas production requires assumptions on which, if any, export and internal pipeline projects will prove economically and geopolitically feasible in the light of all factors referred to above.

These layers of uncertainty yield a very wide range of possibilities for Caspian gas production, with a lower limit defined by local needs plus, presumably, some exports to Ukraine, and an upper limit defined by the most optimistic assumptions conceivable on export market and price developments and the level of competition that Caspian producers will face, and the additional assumption that infrastructural constraints will melt away as needs for pipelines arise. One could go further and just consider how fast the Caspian states' portfolios of fields and prospects could be developed to their estimated full potential, or – as one writer[15] does, for illustrative purposes – assume an r/p ratio of nine years for all of them (this is the ratio of the United States and the United Kingdom) to arrive at several hundreds of bcm a year.

Adopting the less visionary approach of a judicious combination of individual Caspian country authorities' own projections, various Western analysts' viewpoints and my own estimates of current and likely future markets for Caspian produces the estimates shown in Table 4.

Table 4: Future gas production assumptions (bcm)

	2000	2005	2010
Armenia	0.0	0.0	0.0
Azerbaijan	7.0	10.0	18.0
Georgia	0.5	1.0	2.0
Kazakstan	9.0	15.0	24.0
Kyrgyzstan	0.1	0.15	0.2
Tajikistan	0.1	0.15	0.2
Turkmenistan	55.0	70.0	90.0
Uzbekistan	53.0	58.0	65.0
Total	124.7	154.3	199.4

Sources: National authorities, consultants, international financial institutions, own estimates.

In 1993 the Turkmen government adopted a long-term programme for the petroleum sector, envisaging an increase in gas production to 130 bcm in 2000 and 230 bcm a year by 2020. The programme was slightly revised in 1995–6 but the target for 2020 remains as high as 220 bcm. Although much can happen over more than two decades,

---

[15] Joseph P. Riva, Jr.

such optimism appears unfounded. It is not at all clear that gas reserves could support a production of over 200 bcm a year, and the costs of supplying Turkmen gas to distant markets, the probable future level of competition in those markets, and of course geopolitics, present formidable hurdles. However, if the market constraint on production weakens – that is, if Turkmenistan's traditional customers in the FSU regain their ability to pay for supplies, Russia starts importing Turkmen gas, the reported agreement with Russia allowing for exports via Gazprom pipelines to Europe proves real and lasting, and at least one of the republic's independent export pipeline projects goes ahead – a recovery in output to previous peak rates of some 90 bcm a year could perhaps be accomplished over a 10–15-year period.

Russia's VNIIgaz may not subscribe even to this more moderate projection. VNIIgaz researchers hold that considering the degree of depletion of most of Turkmenistan's key producing fields, and given a set of perhaps conservative but not extreme assumptions on discoveries and field developments in the years ahead, geologically possible production in the period 1997–2005 averages only 65 bcm a year. Output could be increased to an average of 75 bcm a year only by intensifying exploration, bringing a maximum of new fields onstream, somehow dealing with hydrogen sulphide and other problems, and working producing fields to the point where output would start declining as early as 2001.

Kazak gas output developments to 2010 will mainly reflect the pace at which Karachaganak is developed, which in turn will depend on the outcome of negotiations over access to Gazprom pipelines, and eventually on whether domestic gas market developments appear to justify large-scale field and pipeline investments. Some time ago the Kazak government presented a plan to increase gas output to 8.5 bcm in 1997, 15.4 bcm in 2000, 28 bcm in 2005 and 36.1 bcm in 2010.[16] These targets reflect hopes for Karachaganak that have proved unrealistic, and now appear far too optimistic; perhaps production can be increased from to today's 5 bcm a year to 36 bcm a year, but it will take longer than 13 years.

The Uzbek authorities' have forecast gas production by 2000 at 60 bcm a year, and unlike some other Central Asian governments' output growth visions, this one is considered fairly realistic, although the deadline may be missed by a year or two. Looking to 2010, forecasters see further steady if unspectacular growth; there are no giant fields awaiting development, but many medium-sized and smaller ones. The government's success or lack of it in attracting foreign investment in the gas sector will play a key role.

As far as gas production in Azerbaijan is concerned, things will get worse before they get better; key producing fields are in steep decline and no new fields will be

---

[16]*East Bloc Energy*, June 1997.

commissioned in the near future.[17] An important question for the longer term is whether Shah Deniz turns out to be primarily an oil and condensate field or primarily a gas field, and what the companies in charge of developing it will do with the gas. To assume a growth in output to 18 bcm a year by 2010 is to be more optimistic than Socar and implies – since it is difficult to see domestic consumption returning to 18 bcm in 2010 – an expectation that Azerbaijan will become a net gas exporter, most likely to Turkey, sometime between 2005 and 2010. The main reasons for considering such a development are that, first, Azeri gas could be highly competitive in the Turkish market; second, a string of Western oil companies desperately seeking outlets for their associated gas could be both willing and able to make an Azerbaijan–Turkey export pipeline project take off; and, third, for political reasons Turkey could be interested in forging a gas link with Azerbaijan. In fact, if all the pieces in the puzzle fall into place, by 2010 Azerbaijan's gas production could be even higher than 18 bcm a year.

---

[17] However, a UK consultancy estimates that refurbishing the Bakhar field and the shallow portion of the Guneshli field could lead to a doubling of Azeri gas production, and Socar is planning to spend $8 million during 1997 on further drilling in the Bakhar and Bulla Deniz fields in an attempt to realize some of this short-term output growth potential.

4 GAS CONSUMPTION

Gas consumption can be forecast by applying either a so-called bottom-up approach or a so-called top-down approach. In the former case one proceeds from base year gas consumption data which should be highly disaggregated (preferably not only by consumption sector but by industry), by making assumptions on output growth, investments, the introduction of gas-using equipment, the gas efficiency of future vintages of equipment etc. within each sector or industry; thus one arrives at the end, by aggregating sector or industry gas use forecasts, at a national gas consumption prediction. In the latter case one proceeds from an energy consumption forecast, normally derived from a GNP forecast and an energy efficiency prediction, to individual fuel use forecasts by 'spreading' energy use out on individual fuels, normally by assuming that fuel shares will change as a function of relative fuel prices. Both approaches – which can be, and often are, combined – have their merits, but the bottom-up approach is demanding in terms of data and therefore does not lend itself well to FSU fuel use forecasting. In the following paragraphs, therefore, we outline recent energy consumption, energy efficiency and individual use developments to set the stage for some simple top-down reasoning about future energy and gas needs.

Primary energy use, energy intensity

Although energy consumption data for the Central Asian and Caucasian republics are scant and unreliable, and GNP figures equally lacking in quality, existing observations and estimates leave no doubt that:

- Total primary energy use in the area has declined severely since the Soviet Union fell apart;
- GNP has dropped even more severely, implying that the energy intensity of the region has increased;
- Energy and GNP decline rates have varied significantly among countries, reflecting differences in resource endowments, political circumstances and economic policies so that the Caspian area is even more heterogeneous in terms of these variables today than at the beginning of the 1990s.

According to IEA and consultancy data, and as indicated in Table 5, the aggregate total primary energy supply (TPES) of the Caspian states declined from about 187 million barrels of oil equivalent per day (mboe/d) in 1991 to some 139 mboe/d in 1995, i.e., by 26%. Meanwhile their aggregate GDP apparently dropped by 38%, implying an increase in the energy intensity of the region of almost 20%.[18] The republics' commercial energy use per capita in 1994 varied between 572 and 3710 kg of oil equivalent (koe), i.e., by a factor of 6.5, and energy consumption per unit of GDP ranged from 1 to 3.3 koe/US$. In general – and not unexpectedly – those republics that are well endowed with energy resources and are net energy exporters have a higher TPES per capita, and get less mileage in the form of goods and services produced out of their energy use, than those forced to import the bulk of their energy supplies.

Of total 1995 primary energy use – which was some 7% higher than the TPES of Belgium, the Netherlands and Luxembourg taken together – Kazakstan accounted for 42%, Uzbekistan for 31%, Azerbaijan and Turkmenistan for 12% and 7% respectively, and Georgia, Armenia, Kyrgyzstan and Tajikistan together for 8%.

Table 5: Total primary energy supply and GDP, 1991 and 1995

	TPES (1000 toe)		GDP (1993 US$bn)[a]		Change in TPES (%)	Change in GDP (%)	Change in energy intensity (%)
	1991	1995	1991	1995	1991–5	1991–5	1991–5
Armenia	7.89	2.46	18.3	8.3	-69	-55	-31
Azerbaijan	23.03	16.20	27.1	10.7	-26	-61	+78
Georgia	9.59	1.93	21.0	7.9	-80	-62	-47
Kazakstan	72.45	53.66	68.2	46.6	-26	-32	+8
Kyrgyzstan	6.94	3.57	15.6	7.7	-49	-51	+4
Tajikistan	5.30	2.94	7.1	3.1	-45	-56	+27
Turkmenistan	13.30	9.67	17.4	12.3	-27	-29	+3
Uzbekistan	48.40	48.57	62.2	51.1	0	-18	+22
Total	186.90	139.00	236.9	147.7	-26	-38	+19

[a]Converted from national currencies at purchasing power parity rates.

Sources: PlanEcon, Inc., *Energy Outlook for the Former Soviet Republics,* various editions; IEA: *Energy Statistics and Balances of Non-OECD Countries,* various editions.

[18] The estimates of declines in GNP used by most students of energy intensity developments in the FSU may be biased. Some researchers, noting that declines in electricity production and consumption – variables that usually track economic up- and downturns closely – have been smaller than reported declines in GNP, draw the conclusion that the FSU economies have not contracted as severely as has been assumed. Economic activity may have been under-reported for a number of reasons; for instance, existing reporting systems may capture declines in output from state-owned factories better than growth in private, more or less informal activity. If this is correct, energy intensities have not increased as sharply as our figures indicate.

The Caspian FSU republics are energy-inefficient not only relative to the averages for countries at comparable income levels, but also by FSU standards. Tajikistan, Azerbaijan, Kyrgyzstan, Armenia and Georgia, which are classified as low-income economies, used between 35% and 270% more energy per capita, and up to 230% more energy per unit of GDP, than the average for such economies. Uzbekistan, Kazakstan and Turkmenistan are lower-middle-income economies and used 20–140% more energy per capita, and up to 270% more energy per unit of GDP, than the average for their group. In Russia energy use per capita is higher, which is understandable considering differences in climate, but energy use per unit of GDP is significantly lower than in Azerbaijan, Kazakstan and probably also Turkmenistan (see Table 6).

Table 6: Energy indicators, 1994

	TPES/capita (kg of oil equivalent)	TPES/GDP (kg of oil equivalent/US$)
Armenia	667	1.0
Azerbaijan	1414	3.3
Georgia	572	1.4
Kazakstan	3710	3.3
Kyrgyzstan	715	1.1
Tajikistan	642	1.7
Turkmenistan	3198	n.a.
Uzbekistan	1886	2.0
Russia	4038	1.7
Low-income economies	384	1.0
Lower-middle-income economies	1540	0.9
Middle-income economies	1593	0.6
Upper-middle-income economies	1715	0.4
High-income economies	5168	0.2

Source: World Bank, *World Development Report 1996.*

Turkmen data indicate that the level of energy use depends strongly on the level of gas production and exports – in 1993 and again in 1995 when gas production plummeted, energy use also fell, and in 1994 when gas production picked up, energy use also recovered. To some extent this relationship is trivial; gas production and transportation are energy- (i.e., gas-) intensive activities. However, the link also operates via public and private consumption, reflecting the government's budgetary responses to fluctuations in revenues. In 1996 the government responded to the previous year's negative gas output and revenue developments by lowering its welfare state ambitions, introducing charges for electricity and other goods previously supplied free of charge.

Turkmenistan's GDP fluctuated strongly between 1991 and 1995, reflecting – as indicated – the up- and downturns of the gas sector, but it seems to have been some 29% lower at the end than at the beginning of the period. Consequently, the energy intensity of the Turkmen economy apparently increased by about 3% during the first half of the 1990s.

Uzbekistan's total primary energy use hardly changed at all between 1990 and 1995. This performance – unique by FSU standards – reflects natural and historical circumstances and, as noted, government policies which softened the blow to the Uzbek economy from the break-up of the Soviet Union. However, it also indicates that energy is being used less efficiently now than at the beginning of the 1990s; after all, GDP dropped by an estimated 18% from 1991 to 1995, yielding a 22% increase in energy use per unit of GDP.

Armenian and Georgian energy consumption declined dramatically between 1990 and 1995, reflecting in the case of Armenia the war over Nagorno-Karabakh and supply cut-offs, and in the case of Georgia civil strife related to the rise and fall of Zviad Gamsakhurdia and the secessionism of the Ossetes and Abkhaz. Azeri energy consumption held up better in spite of the war with Armenia, reflecting Azerbaijan's position as a major regional energy producer. The energy intensity of the Azeri economy apparently increased by more than three-quarters between 1991 and 1995 as GDP plummeted by much more than TPES. The same happened to some extent in Tajikistan, another economy plagued by civil strife but with considerable indigenous energy production. However, estimates of changes in energy use and economic activity levels in war-ravaged societies like Azerbaijan and Tajikistan should probably be taken as little more than best guesses.

Fuel shares

The Central Asian and Caucasian republics differ strongly from one another also in terms of the structure of their TPES. Whereas Kazakstan and Kyrgyzstan depend on coal for about 60% and 30% of TPES respectively, in the other countries solid fuel's share of primary energy supply ranges from zero to 4%. With the exception of Kazakstan, those countries in the region that produce hydrocarbons on a significant scale also consume mainly oil and gas, with Uzbekistan and Turkmenistan depending on gas for three-quarters and two-thirds of TPES respectively. The smaller countries in the area rely to a higher extent on primary (i.e., hydro) electricity.

Table 7: Fuel shares in total primary energy supply, 1994 (%)

	Coal	Oil	Gas	Primary electricity	Total
Armenia	0.3	27.3	51.4	21.0	100.0
Azerbaijan	0.0	54.1	44.5	1.4	100.0
Georgia	3.7	11.5	70.6	14.3	100.1
Kazakstan	59.1	25.0	13.7	2.2	100.0
Kyrgyzstan	30.9	17.0	24.1	28.8	100.8
Tajikistan	2.7	34.6	25.9	37.6	100.8
Turkmenistan	0.0	35.0	67.2	-2.2	100.1
Uzbekistan	3.8	19.3	75.2	1.6	99.9
Total	26.6	27.2	42.6	3.6	100.0

Source: IEA Secretariat.

Fuel shares have not changed dramatically since the beginning of the 1990s, but some adjustments have taken place. In Kazakstan economic dislocations have triggered minor increases in the use of indigenously produced coal at the expense of oil. The gas share was almost the same in 1995 as in 1991. Turkmenistan has seen an increase in the share of oil products at the expense of that of gas. Oil use has held up better than gas use for a number of reasons: a decline in the gas industry's own gas needs (it takes significantly less electricity and compression to produce and transport 35 bcm than 90 bcm of gas); a decline in other industries' gas use; and the fact that the shutting in of gas production capacity has constrained deliveries to domestic consumers too. In Uzbekistan, steady growth in gas production and a decline in gas exports to neighbouring republics have underpinned an increase in the gas share and corresponding declines in the oil and coal shares. In Kyrgyzstan the share of primary electricity in TPES has increased mainly at the expense of the share of oil, reflecting the fact that hydro power is produced locally while oil products have to be imported. Gas use declined in step with total primary energy use through 1994 but apparently recovered strongly in 1995. In Tajikistan the shares of oil and gas have changed only marginally, with the use of primary electricity increasing relative to the use of coal.

Azerbaijan uses more oil and less gas – in relative terms – today than five or six years ago; declines in indigenous gas production and cuts in gas imports have forced consumers with dual firing capacity to switch to oil. In Armenia and Georgia consumption of gas and primary electricity increased in relative terms in 1991–5 in spite of recurrent problems with supply, as oil products more or less disappeared from the market.

Unfortunately, one cannot assume for forecasting purposes either that the level of energy use in the Caspian republics in 1994 was the desired or equilibrium level, or that fuel shares expressed consumers' preferences under prevailing income and price conditions. When gas and electricity use is not metered and bills are not paid, neither incomes nor the prices of gas and electricity matter much for consumption. This holds out the possibility of drops in demand as and when metering is introduced and billing enforced. On the other hand, when supply is rationed or cut for technical or debt reasons, customers willing and able to pay above the going prices may be as helpless as those unable to pay at all, and this holds out the possibility of increases in demand as and when supply constraints are lifted. Which of these forces will prove the strongest when the Central Asian and Caucasian countries proceed down the road of economic reform and 'normalization' remains to be seen.

Gas use

Turning to gas use, the regional heavyweight is Uzbekistan. Turkmenistan has the largest gas production potential and a very gas-intensive economy, but is small in terms of both population and industrial base; and Kazakstan – the only country in the region with a population even approaching that of Uzbekistan, and with a significantly larger TPES – has a primarily coal-based economy.

Estimates of the sectoral structure of gas consumption in the Caspian states vary strongly across sources, but all observers note that in most countries in the area, a significant share of marketed gas goes to the electricity sector.[19] Thus, in Uzbekistan and Turkmenistan power plants account for 25–35% of national gas consumption. The shares of gas going to industry and the communal/residential sector vary widely; countries such as Turkmenistan and Kazakstan are characterized by large distances between population centres and relatively poorly developed domestic pipeline grids using gas mainly for industrial purposes besides power production, while in more 'compact' countries communal institutions, apartment blocks and service businesses are significant gas users.

In Turkmenistan, the electricity sector accounts for about 35% of total gas use while the gas industry itself takes 10% and other sectors – mainly other industry – the remainder. Of Turkmenistan's six major power plants, five are gas-fired, and the sixth, which burns heavy fuel oil (HFO), accounts for only 0.4% of total installed generating capacity, estimated at about 3.2 GW. The 1,680 MW Mary power plant – the biggest of the thermal power stations – burns some 1.5 bcm a year, and the nearby Mary nitrogenous fertilizer plant, which was put into production in the mid-1980s and has an output of 765,000 tonnes per year, accounts for a high share of industrial demand. A chemicals factory in Chardzhou, the Karakum and Pustyannya

---

[19] See in particular PlanEcon, Inc. (1995) for information on the Central Asian electricity industries and their fuel use.

Table 8: Estimated gas consumption, 1990–5 (bcm)

	1990	1991	1992	1993	1994	1995
Armenia	4.4	4.4	1.9	0.8	0.9	2.2
Azerbaijan	18.3	17.0	14.8	12.3	11.7	7.6
Georgia	5.5	5.5	4.9	3.8	2.6	1.5
Kazakstan	14.5	12.8	18.5	15.1	11.0	9.3
Kyrgyzstan	1.9	1.9	1.8	1.4	0.9	2.5
Tajikistan	1.7	1.7	1.7	1.4	1.1	0.8
Turkmenistan	15.9	14.3	13.2	9.6	9.2	8.2
Uzbekistan	37.9	39.0	41.3	44.4	44.3	43.5
Total	100.1	96.6	98.1	88.8	81.7	75.6

Source: PlanEcon, Inc.

compressor stations and households in Ashgabat and a few other towns are the only other major consumers.[20] By 1992 a little over half of the Turkmen population – 88% of city dwellers and 22% of rural households – had access to gas.

Turkmenistan exports gas-based electricity to Uzbekistan and Kazakstan and is offering to sell electricity to Pakistan, but apart from the fact that Pakistan currently has excess generation capacity, the offer has one snag: transmission lines would have to transit Afghanistan. Another proposal to export electricity to Turkey could conceivably be implemented, but as Turkey has been a small net exporter of electricity (to Azerbaijan) since 1990 and plans to commission another 34 power plants before the turn of the century, such exports are unlikely to become significant in the foreseeable future, if ever.

Kazakstan's gas use is concentrated in the industrialized areas in the southeast and the population centres in the vicinity of the pipeline systems crossing Kazak territory. Because of the vastness of the country, many regions have no access to gas and the share of households in consumption is correspondingly small. The government now expects Tractebel, the Belgian winner of a concession to manage Kazakstan's gas pipelines, to extend the network. Plans include building an 1,800 km line with a diameter of 1,020 mm from Aksay near Karachaganak via Aktyubinsk, Krasny Oktyabrsk, Kustanay and Kokchetav to Akmola, the new cap tal, and a 1,200 km line with a diameter of 720 mm connecting Chelkar north of the Aral Sea with Chimkent in southeast Kazakstan. The estimated cost of these two projects alone (and there are more) amount to US$1.45 billion. Besides planning to bring gas to many more local communities, the Kazak authorities promise to increase gas availability to industry – in particular the metallurgical industry – which has recently suffered from energy and fuel shortages.

[20] *Eastern Bloc Energy*, April 1994.

Whether the newly privatized oil and gas producers which are operated by Western companies will play along remains to be seen.

In Uzbekistan the power industry appears to account for nearly 40% of total gas consumption. Although 43 of Uzbekistan's 52 power plants are hydroelectric plants, they account for only about 15% of total generation. Of the nine thermal stations, all are gas-fired or equipped to burn both gas and coal or gas and heavy fuel oil. In 1994 the fuel mix of these plants was about 70% gas, 20% HFO and 10% coal. The commissioning of a huge gas-fired station currently under construction will increase total installed generation capacity by almost 30% and further tilt fuel use towards gas. Total final gas consumption seems to consist of industrial consumption and communal/residential consumption in fairly equal proportions. Among Uzbek industries, the oil and gas industry itself, the chemicals industry and the building materials industry are particularly big gas consumers.

In Azerbaijan, before gas supply disruptions and administrative rationing started to impact on consumption, about 40% of gas supply went to power generation, with the remainder split fairly evenly among industry, district heating, the residential sector and the commercial/public sector. Eight of the country's twelve power stations are thermal and these eight account for more than 85% of total installed capacity. In the early 1990s, they used fuel oil and gas in more or less equal proportions, but following declines in indigenous gas production, increases in the price of imported gas and rapid accumulation of gas debts, the share of gas in the fuel mix of the power sector fell to less than 25%. Gas is traditionally the main fuel in all end-use sectors except transport. Nearly all industrial boilers are designed to burn gas and about 80% of households are connected to the gas distribution pipeline system. However, the implementation of the 1995 decision to stop importing gas from Turkmenistan has led to dramatic declines in both industrial and residential gas use outside the capital and the Sumgait area.

Projections

Even the top-down approach to energy and fuel use forecasting calls for more data than students of the Caspian states currently have at their disposal. Econometric analysis of time series data cannot be carried out since Caspian data from before 1991 are lacking in detail and of dubious quality, and would in any case not have provided much of a guide to the future; in Soviet times energy use was administered from the top whereas in the future consumption will, presumably, reflect consumers' adaptation to changes in income levels, prices and other parameters. It is possible to model energy demand by means of data from after 1991 and making assumptions on elasticity and other parameter values lifted from econometric studies on other countries and regions. However, there are a number of problems with this approach:

- Data on the Caspian countries' energy use and GDP post-independence appear as uncertain as those from the years leading up to independence; besides, even reliable snapshots of current energy consumption levels and patterns would have been snapshots of disequilibrium situations requiring adjustments to become credible as base year data.
- The applicability of parameter values reflecting other countries' circumstances can never be assured.
- Total final consumption data disaggregated by sector, without which the implications of assumed structural change patterns cannot be examined, are still generally lacking.

Grappling with these problems further with a view to building an energy model for the Caspian FSU republics is beyond the scope of this paper. Time and resources allow only for some checking of the implications of a set of assumptions on a few key determinants on gas use variables. However, even simple 'if so' reasoning can, provided the 'ifs' make sense, shed light on the orders of magnitude involved.

Any particular country's use of any particular fuel in any particular year is by definition equal to the product of the country's GDP, the energy intensity of its economy and the share of the fuel in its total energy consumption in that year.

Thus, the rate of change in the use of a particular fuel in any year can be expressed as the sum of the rates of change in GDP, the energy intensity of the economy and the share of that fuel in total energy consumption in that year.

Each of these rates of change has a multitude of determinants. Economic growth reflects factors such as population growth and productivity growth, and the latter factor depends in turn on – among other things – the levels of investments and savings, technological developments and the direction and pace of structural change processes. The amount of energy needed to produce a unit of GDP may decline as a result of energy savings following, for instance, market- or policy-driven energy price increases, when resources are moved from heavy industry to light industry and the service sector and when energy-inefficient buildings and machines are replaced by energy-efficient ones. Evidently, the energy intensity of an economy may increase if one or more of these processes is reversed or – as has happened in the FSU republics – if factories remain lit and heated although production activities grind to a halt. The shares of different fuels in TPES and TFC may change as a result of relative fuel price changes, growth in disposable incomes allowing consumers to switch from less to more convenient fuels, environmental policies and, again, underlying structural change processes.

Ideally, these and other factors should be examined separately and rigidly at consumption sector level. However, with our simple top-down approach we confine ourselves to a discussion of what could be reasonable assumptions on economic growth, the sensitivity of energy consumption to economic growth and the gas share of energy consumption in individual Caspian FSU republics in the years ahead.

The economies of the four gas producers – and biggest gas consumers – in the Caspian appear to have bottomed out and started to recover.[21] Azerbaijan is finally seeing an inflow of foreign oil money, and the Azeri government is enacting reform policy measures. In Kazakstan, small-scale privatization is almost completed and a voucher-based mass privatization programme for larger state enterprises is being implemented. With respect to Kazakstan, the project to create a new outlet for Tengiz oil and possibly Karachaganak condensate is finally moving, and the Kazak government appears committed to reforms and an open-door policy towards foreign investors. Although ongoing and planned projects may suffer further setbacks, it seems a reasonable assumption that the late 1990s and the first decade of the next century will see significant oil-led growth in both Azerbaijan and Kazakstan.

Of Turkmenistan's gas export pipeline projects, only the building of a pipeline to northern Iran is going ahead. The Turkmen government is proceeding only slowly with economic reform and has gained a reputation for not paying sufficient attention to foreign investors' needs. Consequently, although some foreign companies are taking the chance on the republic, it is not seen as standing before a major foreign-investment-led economic upswing. On the other hand, Turkmenistan's gas exports outside the FSU via Russia could be restarted, and exports to Ukraine and other FSU markets will generate more revenues as these republics regain their ability to pay. This alone could provide for considerable economic growth. And in the longer term, perhaps at least one major export pipeline project could be realized.

The outlook for Uzbekistan's economy is not only or primarily a matter of the outlook for its oil and gas sector. The fuel industry accounted in the early 1990s for some 4% of total industrial output. (In Turkmenistan, by contrast, the share of fuels in industrial output was about 25%.) Uzbekistan's fortunes will depend as much on its agriculture and other industry, on whether the government succeeds in exploiting Uzbekistan's location to foster a strong transportation and communications sector, and evidently on the scope and pace of economic reforms. Opinions on the soundness of Uzbek economic policies vary; as noted in Chapter 3, recent reversals of lib-

---

[21] The EBRD reports in its April 1997 *Transition Report Update* the averages of half a dozen forecasters' projections of economic growth in the CIS states in 1997, at 2% for Kazakstan, 4.1% for Turkmenistan, 2.2% for Uzbekistan and 5.5% for Azerbaijan.

eralization policy could indicate that structural problems have been insufficiently addressed, providing for only modest economic growth into the next century.[22]

The Armenian and Georgian economies could enjoy several years of high economic growth because they contracted so severely during the first half of the 1990s that output no longer reflects resources in any meaningful way, because of internal political stabilization and their leaders' embrace of reform policies and – in the case of Georgia – as a consequence of the plan to export a portion of Azeri 'early oil' via Supsa. Kyrgyzstan is ahead of its neighbours in terms of economic reform; it has tried to project itself as a haven of order and reform-mindedness in Central Asia in order to attract foreign investment, but so far without much success, as the country is better endowed with dilapidated heavy industry than with resources of interest to investors. Steady but unspectacular economic growth seems to be the most widely held expectation. Tajikistan, finally, remains in the grip of domestic and regional political unrest and could face further declines in GDP followed by a weak and unsteady recovery.

Next we need assumptions on future changes in the energy intensities of the Central Asian and Caucasian economies – i.e., on the income elasticities of energy use in the area.[23] As noted, the histories of these economies do not provide much guidance, but those of other economies could be of help. When measured over longer periods, ratios between energy consumption growth and economic growth tend to be more stable, in the range between 0.3 and 1.5, similar for countries at the same level of economic development and declining as countries become more developed.

As the Central Asia and Caucasian economies are among those defined as low-income and lower-middle-income by the World Bank, it is tempting to borrow elasticities to forecast their energy use from literature on underdeveloped economies, i.e., higher elasticities than those normally assumed for industrialized countries. However, the processes assumed to provide for a high sensitivity of energy consumption to economic growth in underdeveloped countries – high population growth, rapid urbanization, industrialization – cannot be assumed across the board for the Caspian area. Moreover, the Caspian economies are, as noted, extremely energy-inefficient, reflecting the massive presence of run-down, ineffective industry and an attitude to electricity, heat and gas as basically free goods. Caspian governments are seen as having no alternative to increasing domestic energy and fuel prices

---

[22] For further details on the structure of the economies of the Central Asian republics, see Pomfret (1995).

[23] Strictly speaking, we will not discuss the income elasticity of energy consumption, but a 'composite' elasticity embracing the effects on energy use of energy price movements, non-price driven energy efficiency trends and any other drivers one may think of, as well as the effect of economic growth. As such this elasticity has limited explanatory power, and is just a 'handle' suitable for back-of-the-envelope calculations.

in real terms and improving metering and payment collection arrangements (see below). Meanwhile resources will flow from more to less energy-intensive activities – the shake-out of inefficient, loss-making enterprises that most observers consider inevitable has hardly started – and more energy-efficient equipment will trickle into industries and commercial and household sectors as an aspect of the investment process itself, irrespective of measures to promote energy savings. For these reasons, observers tend to think that energy consumption will be fairly unresponsive to economic growth in the years ahead, possibly following a period of catching up as supply constraints on energy use are lifted.

Fuel shares have not changed dramatically since the early 1990s and there seems to be no reason to expect major upheavals in the years ahead either. The share of electricity in final energy consumption will increase everywhere, but the proportions of hydro, nuclear and thermal power generation in total power generation may remain broadly the same. There are no nuclear power stations in Central Asia and no plans to build any. Hydro power stations in 1994 accounted for only 12% of total electricity generation in Kazakstan, Turkmenistan, Uzbekistan and Azerbaijan, and as electricity demand grows this share will probably decline rather than increase.[24] In Kyrgyzstan and Tajikistan hydro stations in 1994 accounted for 87% of total generation, and as waterfalls are these states' only significant energy resource, here the share of thermal power will probably decline rather than increase. Armenia possesses the only nuclear power plant in the area; it was closed in 1989 following a major earthquake but restarted in 1995 as an emergency measure to cope with extreme energy supply problems. As and when oil and especially gas again become available, incremental electricity demand could be supplied from thermal stations. Georgia has a mixed gas- and hydro-based electricity supply system and is, with untapped hydro resources as well as hopes for improved access to gas, likely to continue relying on both types of capacity.

As for the composition of fossil fuel use, Kazakstan is the only republic in the area using significant amounts of coal. In recent years production has declined, partially owing to supply-side factors. Given the state of mines, the environmental effects of coal burning, the convenience premiums placed by most end-use consumers on other fuels, and the Kazak government's intentions of making gas available to regions which today are without supply, the future will probably see some substitution of gas for coal.

Turkmenistan, Uzbekistan and Azerbaijan consume mainly oil and gas. For Turkmenistan it is expected that the share of gas in TPES will climb back to the lev-

---

[24] Opportunities for imports of hydro electricity from Kyrgyzstan and/or Tajikistan could arise, but pobably not to such an extent as to cut deeply into demand for thermal power.

els of the early 1990s. The government intends to make gas available to the entire population, and is considering further gas-based industrialization such as building a polyethylene plant with a capacity of 200,000 tonnes a year[25] and further gas-based power generation with a view to exporting electricity to other Central Asian republics, Turkey and Pakistan. It is assumed that Uzbekistan will increase its oil use moderately relative to its gas use. In Azerbaijan the share of gas in TPES could increase, though industrial gas use is likely to stagnate or even fall in absolute terms as the republic's obsolete heavy industry contracts, and as residential consumption is constrained by a political decision to stop importing Turkmen gas. Gas use will pick up as and when this constraint is lifted and the power sector, which has been forced by circumstance and against economic and environmental logic to switch from gas to fuel oil, will probably switch back.

The gas price factor

Generally, the outlook for energy prices figures prominently in energy consumption forecasts, and the outlook for gas prices relative to other fuel prices plays a key role in gas use projections. Moreover in the Caspian republics, energy and individual fuel price developments will affect energy growth rates and fuel consumption patterns, and as prices by and large will have to be increased in real terms – governments cannot continue subsidizing consumption for ever, at least not to current extents – clearly price changes will have a dampening effect on consumption growth rates. However, it is not easy to predict either how quickly and decisively price adjustments will be enacted, or the strength and time profiles of their impacts.

Accurate and timely information on end-user prices of gas in the FSU republics is hard to come by. The World Bank reports prices for Azerbaijan, Kazakstan and Uzbekistan dating from the period mid-1995 to mid-1996, and figures for Turkmenistan dating from 1993.[26] Residential customers in Azerbaijan, Turkmenistan and Uzbekistan were charged 0.12–0.15 US cents per cubic metre while Kazak households had to pay 4.20 US cents per cu.m. Industry and power plants were charged US cents 0.24/cu.m in Turkmenistan, 1.84/cu.m in Uzbekistan, 2.36/cu.m (industry) and 5.33/cu.m (power plants) in Azerbaijan, and 8.37/cu.m in Kazakstan. The same source estimates gas production costs in Turkmenistan at US cents 1.8/cu.m. Thus, in Azerbaijan, Turkmenistan and Uzbekistan prices for residential customers did not come close to covering even production costs, let alone transportation and distribution costs, and in Turkmenistan and Uzbekistan too indus-

[25] World Bank, 1994.
[26] Kubota (1996).

trial customers were subsidized over the budget. Only in Kazakstan did prices approach supply costs, and even there households paid less than industrial consumers despite the fact that supply costs were much higher for the residential sector than for other sectors.

By way of comparison, in Turkey in late 1995 households and power plants paid about US cents 18 and 15 per cubic metre of gas respectively.[27]

Afraid of stoking inflation and triggering social unrest, FSU governments often try to delay and dilute the price adjustments they are being advised to carry out by institutions such as the World Bank. As and when they finally do raise prices, responses may be weak because metering and billing systems do not transmit price signals effectively to customers and/or because customers are not in the habit of paying their bills. In most FSU republics, systems whereby residential customers pay symbolic gas bills calculated on the basis of family and apartment size and built into the rent are being replaced with systems linking charges to actual gas consumption, and increasingly sanctions against non-paying industrial customers such as depriving them of gas until they pay are being enacted, but these are costly, politically difficult and thus always slow processes.

We address below the problems of modelling price effects on fuel consumption by a judicious reduction in income elasticities from the time price effects are assumed to kick in – a popular if methodically unimpressive approach.

Combining the assumptions illustrated in Table 9 yields an increase in the eight Central Asian and Caucasian republics' combined gas use from about 78 bcm in 1996 to some 85 bcm in 2000, 96 bcm in 2005 and 108 bcm in 2010; that is, an increase of about 2.5% a year on average. Individual republics' shares in total regional gas consumption change as a result of the assumed increases in the availability of gas and pursuit of gasification policies in certain countries; thus, the Kazak share is seen as jumping from 12 to 18% and the Azeri share from 10 to 13%, while the Uzbek share falls from 54 to 45%.

One could develop any number of scenarios by means of this simple framework. Such exercises would quickly become uninteresting. One example will suffice: keeping the ratio of gas consumption growth to economic growth stable at 0.7 – certainly a possible value – provides for a gas use of 89 bcm in 2000, 107 bcm in 2005 and 132 bcm in 2010. A slower decline in the sensitivity of energy consumption growth to economic growth could reflect lower levels of investment and thus lower economic growth, implying that gas use might not increase much faster in this case than in our base case after all, but the ratio could remain high for other reasons too.

---

[27] IEA: *Energy Prices and Taxes*, fourth quarter 1996.

Table 9: Assumptions on factors determining gas use, 1996–2010 (% per year)

	Average annual growth in GDP (%)	Increase in TPES per 1% growth in GDP (%)	Gas share of TPES (%)
Armenia	4.9	Declining from 0.8 to 0.4	Increasing from 51 to 55
Azerbaijan	6.4	Declining from 0.5 to 0.3	Increasing from 55 to 60
Georgia	5.6	Declining from 0.8 to 0.4	Declining from 71 to 60
Kazakstan	5.4	Declining from 0.7 to 0.3	Increasing from 16 to 24
Kyrgyzstan	3.8	Declining from 0.7 to 0.5	Declining from 35 to 30
Tajikistan	1.4	Declining from 1.0 to 0.7	Declining from 26 to 24
Turkmenistan	4.6	Declining from 0.5 to 0.4	Increasing from 68 to 73
Uzbekistan	3.7	Declining from 0.7 to 0.3	Declining from 75 to 65

Sources: Consultants, own estimates.

Another fairly obvious, but not trivial, conclusion is that what really matters to gas consumption in the Caspian area is how the Uzbek economy fares and what kind of policies on energy and gas use the Karimov administration implements. Increasing economic growth in Uzbekistan by 2% p.a. throughout the forecast period while holding all other parameter values constant yields a 5.5 bcm increase in total regional gas consumption in 2010. By contrast, racking up economic growth in Kyrgyzstan, Tajikistan, Armenia and Georgia by 2% a year yields a mere 1.7 bcm increase in total gas consumption in 2010. The Kazak economy is bigger than the Uzbek one, but Kazakstan uses comparatively little gas. Turkmenistan is historically a bigger gas producer than Uzbekistan, but with its small population and industrial base is no match in terms of gas consumption.

Combining the gas production assumptions for the eight Central Asian and Caucasian republics presented in Chapter 2 and the demand scenarios developed above yields a growth in net gas exports outside the region from 18 bcm in 1995 to about 40 bcm in 2000, 58 bcm in 2005 and 92 bcm in 2010. In other words, a scenario where Caspian gas output increases to 199 bcm and regional consumption to 108 bcm in 2010 can be maintained only if one believes that there could be solvent demand outside the region for more than 90 bcm of Caspian gas a year, and the possibility of the infrastructure to supply this demand. If either (or both) of these requirements seems unfulfillable, something will have to give.

5 EXPORT MARKETS FOR CASPIAN GAS

The questions of where Caspian gas could be marketed, how fast markets will grow and against whom the Caspian FSU republics will have to compete are crucial to an understanding of the economic – as opposed to the geological and technical – potential for Caspian gas production.

In principle, there are no limits to where Caspian gas could be marketed. Pipelines with a capacity of some 28 bcm a year each move Siberian gas thousands of kilometres to European markets. Similar lines could move Caspian gas to Europe, the Indian subcontinent, China and even East Asia. A line to a liquefied natural gas (LNG) ocean terminal would bring the rest of the world within reach. Economically, however, there are constraints on Caspian actors' freedom of choice as regards export strategy. To realize the area's more ambitious gas export projects may need gas prices in excess of current prices. Investors are thus being asked to gamble on a tightening of export markets during the years it will take to get fields and pipelines up and running. Moreover, unit transportation costs decrease with volume, favouring the largest suppliers, and increase disproportionally with transportation distance for piped gas, with a corresponding decrease in distance for LNG, with which Caspian piped gas in many cases would have to compete.

Gas consumption is forecast to increase faster than other energy consumption in both Europe and Asia, for well-documented efficiency and environmental reasons. However, price increases are far from certain. In most markets, gas prices remain linked to oil prices, and oil companies generally expect little or no increase in real oil prices between now and 2010–15. Moreover, potential gas supply seems to be increasing even faster than demand, implying the risks of gas-to-gas competition and a marginalization of market-value gas pricing that could put real gas prices on a declining trend.

General gas market liberalization giving rise to gas-to-gas competition is not a foregone conclusion; probably some countries looking to the United States and the United Kingdom will move fairly quickly towards third party access (TPA) to pipelines and the other features of competitive markets, while others will proceed at a slower pace. Uneven and unpredictable processes of change do not, however, necessarily mean extended windows of opportunity for new suppliers. The longer gas markets remain dominated by a small number of long-term contracts, the longer will gas spot markets remain tiny or non-existent, leaving gas sellers who have no contracts with a volume risk in addition to the price risk.

Below we look briefly at the markets that have figured most prominently in discussions on Caspian area gas: first those in which the Caspian republics already have positions – i.e., the other FSU republics and central and eastern Europe; next, two gas-consuming neighbours (Turkey and Iran); then western Europe; and finally the Asian markets.

Ukraine and Russia

In the 1970s and 1980s Central Asian – primarily Turkmen – gas played an important, if secondary, role in the centrally directed provision of fuel to power plants and end-users in the Soviet Union. The break-up of the Soviet Union did not put an end to this situation as Turkmenistan continued to produce much more gas than could be consumed domestically, and remained constrained in its choice of export strategy by the existing infrastructure. Although the other FSU republics are currently markets of last resort, cash-strapped markets are better than no markets, and in the longer run payment problems could become less severe and a position in a big market such as Ukraine a valuable asset. Thus, although Caspian gas in the future may flow to many destinations, probably a large share of it will continue to go to other FSU republics, with Ukraine and possibly Russia at the top of the list.

Ukraine

Ukraine is a big country using energy in inefficient ways. Its energy consumption structure reflects years of systematic substitution away from other fuels to gas; indigenous gas production covers only one-fifth of needs and until recently it had no alternatives to sourcing its gas imports from Russia and Turkmenistan. In 1990 gas consumption was about 115 bcm, corresponding to about 36% of TPES. Over the next five years consumption of gas declined to an estimated 73 bcm but its share of energy use increased to 41%. Gas needs declined as GNP shrank by more than 50%, and gas availability declined as indigenous production dropped and imports were hit by Russia's and Turkmenistan's post-independence gas pricing policies.

In late 1995 the International Energy Agency predicted, under moderately optimistic assumptions on reform policies and economic growth, that Ukrainian gas use would recover to about 83 bcm in 2000 and 110 bcm in 2010. The Ukrainian authorities very optimistically project gas production by 2010 at 35.5 bcm, but most independent analysts consider that just stabilizing output at around 20 bcm a year will take considerable effort. Thus, import needs could be nearly 90 bcm a year in 12–15 years' time.

Both Russia and Turkmenistan started in 1992 to charge 'world level prices' – typically, $80 per 1,000 cubic metres – for their gas exports to other FSU republics. Debts have mounted, leading to cuts in deliveries. Russian–Ukrainian skirmishes over gas payment terms and arrears have on a couple of occasions led to drops in pipeline pressure levels at the Ukrainian–Slovak and Ukrainian–Romanian borders, and are well documented. However, Turkmen–Ukrainian clashes have been more severe: at one point Turkmenistan halted deliveries of gas to Ukraine for a full seven months.

By April 1997 Kiev had run up gas debts to Ashgabat of almost $1.1 billion. There were conflicting reports as to whether arrears were still rising or had started to come down. Ukraine, whose debts to Gazprom are even higher, has been unable to pay for gas supplies mainly because the Ukrainian enterprises involved in gas import and distribution make little money. A high share of the industrial users that are their main customers habitually ignore their gas bills. The worst offenders are Minenergo, the state holding company for the electricity sector, and the Ministry of Industry. Advisers urge the Ukrainian government to raise prices, improve metering and billing of gas consumption and authorize supply cut-offs to force customers who have the money but consider gas a free good to pay up. The government is moving, but slowly.

The Ukrainian authorities have strongly criticized the Russian decision to build a new export pipeline across Belarus and Poland to Germany, arguing that Ukraine is ready to transit much more Russian gas than it currently does, and taking steps to upgrade key transit pipelines. If Kiev persuades Gazprom to route a large share of incremental gas exports to Europe via Ukraine, and Gazprom persuades Kiev to continue taking payment for transit services in gas rather than cash, Ukraine's incremental gas needs could be covered, more or less, for the foreseeable future.

The Kuchma government has nonetheless signalled an interest in diversifying gas imports, and by the end of 1996 an agreement providing for delivery of 6–10 bcm of Uzbek gas during 1997 was announced. Ukrainian leaders have also held exploratory talks with Iran. One plan stipulates the building of a pipeline from Iran via Azerbaijan and Russia to Ukraine. Another idea is to build one or two spurs to Ukraine from the planned pipeline from Iran via Turkey to Europe. Such a pipeline could conceivably also carry Central Asian gas. The former of these projects has the flaw that the line would have to cross Russian territory, implying Gazprom's, participation and control; the latter presupposes the existence of a line that remains on the drawing board; and both face the hurdle represented by the state of the parties' finances and the difficulties of funding projects with Iranian participation. Moreover, neither Iran nor any other new supplier can be expected to offer Ukraine softer terms than Russia has done.

Since 1995 the Ukrainian authorities have experimented with gas import liberalization, but reforms have been opaque and appear to have been driven by a desire to

56

confuse creditors and stave off further cuts in supplies of imported gas while delaying more painful measures, rather than by a desire to put the supply system on a sounder footing. In the past, Ukrgazprom, a state-owned joint stock company, had a monopoly on gas imports and transmission. Currently, half a dozen private or corporatized trading companies handle the bulk of imports from Gazprom, Turkmenistan and Uzbekistan. This arrangement has allowed the Ukrainian authorities to maintain that they now bear no responsibility for the continued accumulation of debts. However Turkmenistan's President Niyazov has called their bluff, suggesting that if the intermediaries are the problem they should be relieved of their duties and the gas trade be re-established on an intergovernmental basis. In March 1997 President Kuchma fired the head of the Ukrainian State Oil and Gas Committee, citing the failure of the new system to stem the accumulation of debts. Apparently the responsibility for importing Turkmen gas is to be given back to Ukrgazprom. These developments indicate a growing awareness among the Ukrainian leadership that there are no quick fixes to the republic's gas supply problems, but the consequences for reform policies remain to be seen.

Russia

Russia is shaping the Caspian republics' chances of becoming significant gas producers and exporters in a number of ways – as an investor and partner in field development and pipeline projects, as a transit country for their exports to other FSU republics and eventually Europe, as a competitor in most of these markets, and as a market in its own right.

Currently, the Central Asian republics export limited amounts of gas to Russia as a matter of expediency and necessity; they would have preferred to sell it elsewhere if possible. Turkmenistan and Kazakstan both strive to gain access to Gazprom's export pipelines to Europe while trying to raise money to build their own export pipelines to non-FSU markets. The future, however, may well see an upswing in Russia's need for Central Asian gas, and if the establishment of interrepublican gas trade on commercial terms proceeds apace, Gazprom could emerge as no less attractive a customer than the European gas-importing companies.

Such a scenario is rendered plausible by Gazprom's plans to increase its exports to Europe from 112.5 bcm in 1995 to some 200 bcm a year by 2010.[28] Gazprom expects an increase in Europe's gas use from 406 bcm in 1995 to around 600 bcm in 2010 and intends to capture almost half of this incremental market for itself.

---

[28] See Stern (1995), and his 'Gas in Russia: Revisiting the Supply Side', in *Gas Matters*, December 1996, for further details about Gazprom's export plans and supply options.

Turkmenistan and Kazakstan could be called upon to play parts in this scheme as suppliers of relatively cheap gas to southern Russia, allowing Gazprom to export a higher share of output from producing and new fields in the Nadym-Purtaz region in Western Siberia and to delay the planned development of the Yamal Peninsula's on- and offshore fields.

The offshore fields – Bovanenko, Kharasavey and Kruzenshtern – would be technically challenging, costly and risky to bring onstream as lead times would be so long as to create great uncertainty over Gazprom's assumptions at the time of project start-up on the eventual size of the European gas market and the rules of the game and level of competition there. Postponing the decision to go ahead would, therefore, make sense.

Supplementing Russian production with Central Asian gas is not the only alternative to forging ahead at Yamal, but probably the cheapest one. It would also seem to support an overall Russian strategy of economic reintegration of the CIS. Jonathan Stern estimates Russian imports of Central Asian gas by 2010 at anything between zero and 60 bcm, while Michael Korchemkin estimates that if Russia decides to increase supply in this way, imports of Central Asian gas could amount to 39 bcm a year in 13 years' time.[29]

Central and eastern Europe

The central and east European countries are scaling down their trade with the FSU in order to do more business with other areas. Although network-bound energy trade patterns are among the hardest to break, most of the countries have expressed an interest in diversifying gas imports. Central Asian gas could complement if not replace Russian gas, and if, imported via pipelines outside Gazprom's control, could both trigger some price competition and provide for added security of supply. As for their competitiveness, the Central Asian states might be more willing than other potential suppliers to consider barter arrangements – still an important consideration for at least some east European states. For its part, Russia might be more willing to yield shares of its central and east European markets than of its west European ones, in order to consolidate its hold on the Caspian states' gas industries and extract political concessions; thus, the recent Gazprom offer to reintroduce a Turkmen quota of total FSU gas exports was limited to exports to central and eastern Europe.

In 1995 the six largest central and eastern European states[30] consumed a total of 69.7 bcm of gas, and imported 58% of supply, that is, a total of about 40 bcm.[31]

---

[29] Korchemkin; Stern (see notes 13 and 28 above).
[30] Bulgaria, the Czech Republic, Hungary, Poland, Romania and Slovakia.
[31] Cedigaz.

Consumption could increase to 100–110 bcm a year between 1995 and 2010, and as regional gas production is likely to remain on a declining trend, import needs could increase to 70–90 bcm a year.

Currently, Caspian gas can only reach eastern and central Europe via Gazprom's export pipelines running via Ukraine to the Czech and Slovak republics and onward to Germany, and via Ukraine and Moldova to Romania and Bulgaria. As noted, these lines have limited spare capacity, and various potential bottlenecks must be removed quickly to allow for envisaged increases in flows.

Traditionally, the central and east European states have imported Russian gas under intergovernmental arrangements with Russia linked to their contributions towards the development of the Orenburg and Yamburg fields, and not under regular, Western-style long-term take-or-pay contracts. A low share of projected demand in 2010 is contracted for, meaning that a correspondingly high share is up for grabs. These countries thus attract strong interest from Russia, which intends to hold on to its old markets, if necessary on updated terms, as well as from other established suppliers to western Europe, and from newcomers.

For this very reason, the windows of opportunity may not remain open for very long. Poland, which could become the transit country for a large share of incremental Russian gas exports, recently signed a long-term take-or-pay contract with Gazprom for delivery of 250 bcm over a 25-year period, and has also signed a letter of intent with the Dutch gas company Gasunie to import 2 bcm a year of Dutch gas – or, actually, Russian gas, but carrying a Gasunie guarantee – from 1999 or 2000. The Polish gas company POGC is also considering imports of Norwegian gas, and the building of an LNG terminal at Gdansk. In Hungary, Panrusgaz – a joint venture owned by the national oil and gas company MOL and Gazprom – has signed a 20-year contract with Gazprom stipulating delivery of a total of 225 bcm, with the gas set to arrive via Austria as well as Ukraine. Hungary has also contracted for supplies via the new HAG (Hungary-Austria) pipeline from Ruhrgas and Gaz de France.

Serving as transit countries for the bulk of Russia's gas exports to Europe, the Czech Republic and Slovakia pay less than countries further downstream for Russian gas, i.e., below or at the lower end of the range of west European import prices. Transport cost advantages represent a strong argument for continuing to work closely with Gazprom. The Czech Republic has contracted with Norway for delivery of a total of 53 bcm over 20 years, but will probably also sign a long-term contract with Gazprom; the Czech authorities responded to Russian criticism of their deal with Norway by ensuring that Gazprom will remain the republic's main gas supplier. The Slovak authorities do not seem interested in even a symbolic diversification of imports; in late April 1997 the Slovak and Russian ministers signed a 10-year gas supply contract providing for delivery of as much gas as the republic will need during the contract period, and the Slovak leaders made no concessions in a public debate on the security of gas supply and the virtues of import diversification triggered by the Czechs' signing of a contract with Norway.

If any one of the plans to build independent pipelines from the Caspian area via Turkey to Europe is realized, Bulgaria and Romania would for locational reasons seem the most likely takers of Caspian area gas among the central and east European states. However, they are not sitting and waiting for Caspian gas either. Currently, they import gas exclusively from Russia, and diversification plans are at an early stage. Neither country has much to offer to the West, hard currency to spare, or room for manoeuvre in reorienting its trade. At the same time, both play important parts as transit countries in Gazprom's plans to capture a high share of incremental eastern Mediterranean gas demand. The pipelines carrying Russian gas to Bulgaria continue to Turkey, Greece and Macedonia, a decision has been made to construct a line from Bulgaria to Serbia, and in the future Russian gas could flow along this southern route all the way to Italy. Thus, old relationships of mutual dependence between Bulgaria and Romania on the one side and Russia on the other seem to be strengthening rather than the opposite.

The Romanian authorities are considering import diversification projects. There is a plan to build an LNG terminal at Constansa and an intention to tap into the planned pipelines carrying Iranian, Turkmen or Kazak gas via Turkey to Europe as and when any of these pipelines see the light of day. However, a project to build a link to the main pipeline system moving Russian gas through Ukraine so as to achieve at least a diversification of import routes for Russian gas, and another project to build a link to the Hungarian network which would pave the way for access to the European network, are likely to be implemented much sooner. Thus the Central Asian gas producers again have to watch a potential customer cement relations with its current supplier and forge links with others, because for the time being they themselves do not represent an alternative.

Turkey

Turkey plays a key role in the Turkmen authorities' gas export strategy, and the Turkish market is followed closely by the other Caspian gas producers too. The dynamics and potential size of the Turkish gas market make it a prime target for all producers supplying or hoping to supply Europe. Additionally, almost the only way for Caspian gas to reach Europe without crossing Russian territory in Gazprom pipelines is via Turkey.

As yet, Turkey is a minor gas consumer – in 1995 total gas use amounted to 6.4 bcm, corresponding to 9.3% of TPES. But only a decade ago the gas share of TPES was virtually zero. Between 1987 and 1995, consumption increased by an average of 32% a year. Clearly, growth will not continue at this pace. But the Turkish authorities, foreign oil and gas companies and independent observers alike expect further leaps in demand. The Turkish Ministry of Energy and Natural Resources sees total primary energy use increasing by an average of 6.2% a year between 1995 and 2010, i.e., from 63.1 mtoe in 1995 to 155.6 mtoe in 2010, and gas use increasing by an average of 10.5% a year, i.e., to about 31 bcm, which corresponds to 18% of TPES in 2010. And Botas, the national pipeline construction and gas-importing, transmission and distribution company, is making arrangements to supply some 27 bcm in 2000 and 60 bcm a year by 2010.

Currently more than 50% of gas use is accounted for by the electricity sector. Of total final gas use, industry accounts for about 70% and households, commercial enterprises and service institutions for the remainder. There seem to be possibilities for further gasification in all sectors. Although most power plants built in recent years are gas-fired, gas-based power generation still accounts for only about 15% of total power generation. As for industry and households, consumption remains restricted by the size of the transmission and distribution pipeline grids. The one transmission pipeline in operation extends from the Turkish–Bulgarian border via Istanbul, Izmit, Bursa and Eskisehir to Ankara. However, spurs are under construction, and there are plans to bring gas to eastern Turkey as well.

Turkey is an insignificant gas producer – in 1995 the country's seven small gas fields yielded a total of 182 million cubic metres. Remaining recoverable reserves are estimated at 8.7 bcm and TPAO, the national upstream oil and gas company, aims only at maintaining output at current levels. Thus, the envisaged massive growth in demand will have to be supplied entirely from imports.

Turkey started importing gas from Russia in 1987 under a contract providing for delivery of 6 bcm a year for 25 years. In 1994 a liquefied natural gas terminal located at Marmara Ereglisi near Istanbul was commissioned, and imports of LNG from Algeria started in the same year. The first contract, signed in 1988, stipulates delivery of 2 bcm a year over a 20-year period, while later contracts provide for total imports of 4 bcm a year from the late 1990s. Recently Botas has been negotiating in all directions for further imports to close the envisaged, rapidly widening gap between projected demand and contracted supply. Currently contracts or memoranda of understanding exist with some ten different suppliers including Russia and Algeria, and no doubt more producers and traders with piped gas or LNG to sell are planning to descend on Ankara.

Russia is aggressively courting Turkish energy decision-makers. In September 1996 Gazprom and Botas signed a memorandum of understanding on increasing deliveries via Bulgaria from 6 to 14 bcm a year, and building a pipeline with a capacity of 9 bcm a year from Russia via Georgia to eastern Turkey. Subsequently Gazprom has proposed to build a pipeline with a capacity of 16–18 bcm a year from Izobilnoye – a compressor station on the pipeline moving Siberian gas to the north Caucasus – to Tuapse on the Russian Black Sea coast and a subsea pipeline onward to Samsun or Trabzon on the northern coast of Turkey.

In August 1996 Iran landed a major gas export contract with the Turkish government, providing for deliveries starting at 3 bcm in 1997 and increasing to 10 bcm a year from 2000 to 2020. The direct value of the project is put at $23 billion. Its indirect value to Iran could be much higher; being seen doing normal business with an OECD country, and above all being trusted to deliver on a contract to supply network-bound energy, could contribute significantly to restoring the Iranian government's international image. Construction of a pipeline to move the gas into eastern Turkey is about to start. Botas has called for bids to build the 300 km segment between the Turkish towns of Dogubeyazit, located close to the Iranian border, and Erzurum, from where a pipeline would be laid to Ankara. Iran will be responsible for building the 270 km segment from Tabriz to the Turkish border.

In early 1986 the presidents of Turkey and Turkmenistan signed a memorandum of understanding for delivery of Turkmen gas to begin at 2 bcm a year in 1998 and increase to 15 bcm a year after 2010. Also in early 1996 the Turkish authorities turned to Iraq for future gas supplies, and during the year a plan took shape to build a 1,380 km pipeline with a capacity of some 10 bcm a year from fields in northeastern Iraq to Anatolia. Finally, Botas has contracted for delivery of the LNG equivalent of 1.2 bcm a year from Nigeria, has signed memoranda of understanding with Egypt for 4 bcm a year and Qatar for 1 bcm a year, and is negotiating with Abu Dhabi, Oman and possibly more suppliers of LNG. A US company has carried out a feasibility study for building a second LNG import terminal at Iskanderun or Izmir.

Observers are now asking themselves which of the signed agreements and memoranda of understanding will actually result in gas deliveries, rather than whether Botas needs to line up even more supplies; there is a strong feeling that Botas' demand forecasts are over-optimistic and that the company has over-contracted.[32]

Turkmenistan would seem to have a fair chance of delivering some gas to Turkey, on the basis of the memorandum of understanding, and given that supplying Turkmen gas to Turkey appears economically feasible. Gas production costs are thought to be around $18 per 1,000 cu.m in Turkmenistan as in the Middle East and Siberia,[33] and transport costs of moving about 7 bcm a year 2,000 km from Central

---

[32] The World Bank expects Turkish gas demand to increase to 11.5 bcm in 2010, i.e., to less than 20% of the level forecast by Botas.

[33] Kubota (1996).

Asia to Turkey are estimated at about $60 per 1,000 cu.m. Meanwhile the costs of coal and fuel oil to Turkish power plants – the fuels that Turkmen gas would have to squeeze out – are put at the equivalent of $127 and $198 per 1,000 cu.m of gas respectively. If Azerbaijan should find itself with gas available for export, transport costs entailed in moving it to Turkey would be even lower, and Azerbaijan's ability to compete on costs correspondingly better.

Iran

Iran has enormous gas reserves, is a major gas producer and could become a major gas exporter and thus a strong competitor to the gas-producing Caspian republics. Nonetheless, and paradoxically, Iran could also absorb significant amounts of its northern neighbours' gas.

Iranian gas consumption is booming. In the mid-1980s the gas share of TPES was about 17%; today it is estimated at 40%. The Iran–Iraq war put a lid on domestic oil product use; after the war, consumption exploded, cutting into crude oil exports and threatening to deprive the state of revenues of some $9–10 billion a year. The Iranian authorities responded by starting to dismantle oil product subsidies and by launching a gasification programme. By 1995 about 220 cities and towns with more than three million homes had access to gas. The National Iranian Gas Company (NIGC) reportedly plans to link up another 65 towns, bringing the number of homes with access to gas to 4.7 million by 1999, and a few years into the next century the gas pipeline grid could cover altogether 350 cities and towns. Total domestic gas use (exclusive of reinjection, flaring and venting) is planned to increase from about 35 bcm in 1995 to 45 bcm in 2000.

At the same time the Iranian oil industry needs increasing amounts of gas for reinjection into its ageing oil fields – in particular the southern Khuzestan onshore fields and the Kharg Island area offshore fields – in order to maintain pressure and output rates. In 1976 plans were presented to boost reinjection to 84 bcm a year, but the revolution and the war made this target unattainable; the government aims at a reinjection rate of 48 bcm a year by the turn of the century, but faces, as always, severe funding problems.[34]

In other words, far from being awash with gas, Iran needs a greater supply than is currently available, and this need will increase in the years ahead if only to keep up oil exports.

The gas pipeline network remains small given Iran's size and gas endowments and ambitions. By 1993 a total of about 4,600 km of transmission pipelines carried

[34] *Gas Matters*, August 1996.

gas from fields in western and southwestern Iran northward to Isfahan, Arak, Qom, Tehran, Qazvin, Rasht, Tabriz and Astara near the Iranian–Azeri border. The backbone of the system is constituted by the Igat-1 and Igat-2 pipelines, built for export purposes but serving mainly domestic customers. The only transmission pipeline apart from this system is one running from the Sarakhs field near the Iranian–Turkmen border westward to the southeastern corner of the Caspian Sea. Building new pipelines from the fields on and off Iran's Persian Gulf coast to customers in eastern and northern Iran that do not yet have access to gas would be very expensive; distances are considerable and the terrain not particularly easy. Thus the gas industry appears to give priority to the building of branch lines to the Igat-1 and Igat-2 based system, distribution lines and the missing links of the east–west line; soon, Iran will be able to offer transportation from its border with Turkmenistan to that with Turkey.

This pipeline will carry Iranian and Turkmen gas to Turkey and be used to import Turkmen gas into northern Iran; the investment and operating costs of supplying Iranian gas to these parts of the country would probably be so high that NIGC can pay as much as anyone is prepared to pay for Turkmen gas and still save money.[35] If gas consumption in northern Iran and/or Iranian gas exports grow quickly, deliveries of Turkmen gas could conceivably become significant. On the other hand, they could also stagnate or come to a halt.

Western Europe

Asian gas markets may have a greater potential for growth, but western Europe[36] continues to hold a special attraction for the Caspian gas-producing states. It accounts for some 16% of world gas consumption, has recently shown remarkable dynamism, with the possibility of windows of opportunity opening for new suppliers, is not too far away, and pays in hard currencies.

West European gas use increased by some 6% – from 330.5 to 350.4 bcm – between 1994 and 1995,[37] and apparently by an amazing 10% between 1995 and 1996.[38] In the United Kingdom, consumption jumped by 16%, and Germany and France saw increases of 12% and 10% respectively. Even in the Netherlands, where gas accounts for more than 40% of TPES, indicating that some market segments

---

[35] Iran will for some years receive Turkmen gas as payment for pipeline building and transit services; thus, for the moment, cash payment and pricing are not key issues.
[36] Defined here as Austria, Belgium, Bosnia-Herzegovina and the Federal Republic of Yugoslavia, Croatia, Denmark, Finland, France, Germany, Greece, Ireland, Italy, Luxembourg, the Netherlands, Norway, Portugal, Slovenia, Spain, Sweden, Switzerland and the United Kingdom
[37] Excluding stock changes. *Source*: Cedigaz.
[38] *Petroleum Economist*, May 1997 (World Gas Conference issue).

could be close to saturation, consumption was up by 7%. Cold weather played a part, but growth rates also reflected further switching to gas both in the power sector and in the residential and commercial sector. In the United Kingdom, price drops related to increased competition for gas customers gave an extra boost to consumption.

Unsurprisingly, there is a fairly wide range of opinion on how fast the west European gas market will grow in the years ahead. The International Energy Agency, in its *1996 World Energy Outlook,* presents two energy consumption scenarios, one characterized by the emergence of oil production capacity constraints and oil price increases and one emphasizing technological developments and energy savings; in the former, western Europe's gas use reaches 460 bcm a year by 2010, while in the latter consumption declines to 340 bcm. DRI/McGraw Hill, Wood Mackenzie and WEFA – three leading consultancies – see demand increasing by 54%, 54% and 50% respectively between 1995 and 2010 in their reference scenarios. Gazprom also appears to subscribe to a consumption growth forecast of about 50%. Western companies are generally more conservative in their expectations; thus, Ruhrgas thinks that gas use will be in the 380–400 bcm range by 2010. Most experts agree that the electricity sector will remain the most dynamic market segment: in the IEA's scenarios to 2010 the share of gas going to power plants increases to between 23 and 36%.

At least the higher of these projections hold out the possibility of openings for Caspian gas in west European markets towards the end of the forecast period. However, deliveries will hardly be on a large scale and may not materialize at all. West European countries have already contracted for all the imported gas they will need at least until 2005, and some countries appear to be fully supplied even further into the future. Assuming extensions of a reasonable share of existing contracts and considering both that established and new gas suppliers are lining up to fill the remaining gap between forecast demand and supply and that Caspian gas would not be a cheap alternative, western Europe may not need to tap into the gas reserves of Turkmenistan, Kazakstan, Uzbekistan and Azerbaijan until much later in the 21st century.

Concerning the competitiveness of Caspian gas, L'Observatoire Méditerranéen de l'Energie in 1995 estimated for the IEA[39] that the costs of supplying Turkmen gas to western Europe would range from $127/1,000 cu.m for deliveries via Iran and Turkey to $152/1,000 cu.m for deliveries via Russia and Ukraine. In comparison, Algerian piped gas could be supplied for $64/1,000 cu.m and Russian gas for $113–131/1,000 cu.m. Moving out the supply curve for new gas, more than 200 bcm could be made available to western Europe before it would be necessary to turn to Turkmenistan.

[39] IEA (1995 b).

Most forecasters explicitly or implicitly assume that the governing principles of the majority of west European gas markets – long-term take-or-pay contracts and indexation of gas prices to oil product prices – will remain in place. And so they may. However, the United States and now the United Kingdom are providing examples of different ways of organizing gas transportation and marketing, the EU Commission is pushing for a liberalization of markets, and big gas users all over Europe including electricity companies, industry and local gas distributors are doing the same. Meanwhile, the network of transmission pipelines is growing denser, and 'hubs' are emerging, making it easier for buyers to shop around for good offers. These and other trends[40] could lead to rapid growth in gas spot markets and instances of gas-to-gas competition, pulling prices down and perhaps allowing for even more rapid growth in gas consumption than has been foreseen. Whether supply will grow in step with demand under such circumstances is another question; defenders of current arrangements hold that E&P will decline in the face of volume in addition to price uncertainty, gradually affecting production, choking off price declines and pushing consumers back towards longer-term contracts.

For some new suppliers, a liberalization of the European gas market could be good news. LNG suppliers and piped gas suppliers with access to pipelines could conceivably capitalize on opportunities for spot sales. However, increased price and volume uncertainty would not make it easier to fund new long-distance pipelines. Thus, the Caspian producers probably have no reason to hope for changes in the rules of the game.

Pakistan and India

The Turkmen authorities and foreign oil and gas companies operating in Turkmenistan are interested in the Pakistani gas market; as noted, two groups of companies are planning to build pipelines from fields in southern Turkmenistan via Afghanistan to Pakistan. This interest is due to the fact that the Pakistani gas market, although not yet very big, is among the world's most dynamic. In 1985 Pakistan used 8.1 bcm of natural gas; ten years later consumption was 18.2 bcm – an average annual growth of 8.4%. Between 1993 and 1996 alone the gas industry implemented a 30–40% expansion of transmission and distribution pipeline networks; 700,000 new connections were allotted. TPES is forecast to grow rapidly and the gas share of energy use, currently 38%, is also expected to increase. The Pakistani authorities think consumption could exceed 40 bcm a year even by the turn of the century, and continue growing at a fast pace.

---

[40] See Stoppard (1996) for a discussion of recent and ongoing changes in the European gas market.

Until now, Pakistan has been self-sufficient in gas. Indigenous production is expected to continue to increase to 28 bcm in 1998. Longer-term production forecasts are not rosy, however; output growth is expected to fall increasingly behind demand growth. The Sui gas field, the world's seventh largest when it went onstream in 1955, and the Mari field, which has been in operation since 1966, are at fairly advanced stages of depletion. The bulk of fields put into production in recent years, under development or slated for development are comparatively small.

Western analysts[41] see Pakistan's gas consumption increasing to about 27 bcm in 2000, 36 bcm in 2005 and 48 bcm in 2010, and indigenous production levelling out in the 27–29 bcm a year range, implying a supply gap opening up only after the turn of the century and increasing to about 20 bcm in 2010. These projections could be too pessimistic from a supply gap point of view. The application of new technology at fields in production could yield higher than expected recovery rates, and recent and planned improvements in investment conditions for foreign oil and gas companies could lead to new discoveries on an unforeseen scale. That has happened in numerous other countries. Moreover, Pakistan has still not seen a lot of exploration – by the early 1990s only 0.42 wells had been drilled per 1,000 square kilometre of basin. The corresponding figures for India, the OPEC countries and the United States were 6, 20 and 301 respectively.[42] On the demand side, if gas price reforms put into effect by the caretaker government that took over in November 1996 are continued, the potential for gas use efficiency improvements could prove to be larger than assumed.

These possibilities aside, there is no lack of gas-producing countries in the vicinity which would like to help alleviate Pakistan's looming gas shortage problems. Both Iran and Qatar in addition to Turkmenistan are promoting pipeline projects. It is clear that Pakistan will not need or be able to support more than one or possibly two of these projects; nor is the Turkmen project the most likely to be realized in terms of costs, external support and political feasibility.

The Indian gas market is the larger prize in the race by producing countries and companies to gain footholds in southwest Asia. In 1995 India used only marginally more gas than Pakistan in spite of its much larger population and economy. But consumption is expected to grow even faster than in Pakistan in the years ahead; as gas use amounts to only 5–6% of total primary energy use, the potential for substitution from other fuels into gas appears considerable, especially in the electricity sector and certain industries. Western analysts forecast consumption at up to 38 bcm in 2000 and 75 bcm in 2010, and local experts are advising the Indian authorities to prepare for gas needs exceeding 100 bcm in 2010. Indigenous production is seen as

[41] The World Bank, IEA, Cedigaz, other sources quoted in Kubota (1996).
[42] Petroleum Economist, *Pakistan & Bangladesh: Their Energy Potential.*

increasing to 21–22 bcm in 2000 and 38–39 bcm in 2010, calling for imports of around 16 bcm in the former year and more than 35 bcm in the latter.

India is currently looking hard for new gas supplies, which could be imported via pipelines from Turkmenistan, Iran, Qatar or Oman and/or as LNG from Middle Eastern, Far Eastern and possibly other sources. The pipeline alternatives are fraught with problems, however. India has strong political and security of supply reservations about receiving a product such as gas via Pakistan. India and Oman have discussed building an offshore pipeline bypassing Pakistani territory, but in 1996 the Omanis declared the project infeasible. A decision was due to be taken after a full technical feasibility study had been submitted. The Turkmen alternative suffers also from instability problems in the other transit country, Afghanistan, and the Iranian alternative from the particular funding problems that arise when Tehran is involved in a project.

According to the World Bank, the export of Central Asian gas to Pakistan and India is economically feasible. The costs of piping gas approximately 2,500 km from Central Asia to Pakistan are estimated at $60–78 per 1,000 cu.m depending on the level of exports, and the costs of sending gas all the way to India – a distance of 3,500 km – are put at $81–109 per 1,000 cu.m on the same assumptions with respect to volumes.[43] At the same time the prices of the fuels that would have to be backed out – fuel oil in Pakistan and coal in India – are the equivalent of $201 and $120 per 1,000 cu.m respectively. The competitiveness of Central Asian gas in the Pakistani and Indian markets is another issue; supply cost differences appear to give Middle Eastern producers the edge in both markets.

China and Japan

Both Turkmenistan and Kazakstan consider gas exports to China an interesting and feasible long-term alternative. From a market perspective they are right to look eastwards. The Chinese gas market remains small; in 1995 consumption amounted to only 16.7 bcm, corresponding to some 1.8% of TPES. However, in the IEA's scenarios to 2010 Chinese gas use increases to 34–52 bcm a year. These growth projections reflect assumptions on high growth in GNP and energy consumption rather than a belief that gas will become a dominant fuel. In both scenarios the gas share of TPES increases, but only to 3.7%. This expectation of only modest switching (from coal) to gas reflects in turn an assumption that gas supply will become an increasingly tight straitjacket on demand. If more gas could be produced or imported at competitive costs, clearly the demand would be there. Pollution problems related to coal burning in power plants, industry and households in urban areas are already

---

[43] Kubota (1996).

68

extreme, and will get worse. The Chinese leadership would probably not hesitate to implement more vigorous coal-to-gas substitution policies if given the opportunity.

Until now China has neither exported nor imported gas. In other words, marketed production in 1995 was also 16.7 bcm. Between 1985 and 1995 production increased by an average of 3.9% a year – that is, less rapidly than consumption is forecast to increase. Proven reserves amount to 2,060 bcm, implying a reserves-to-production ratio of over 120 years, but a high share of undeveloped reserves is located in inhospitable areas far away from consumption centres. Incremental demand will therefore have to be supplied, observers think, by a combination of incremental indigenous production and imports. With respect to local output, in 1994 a $1 billion rehabilitation and upgrading programme was announced for the Sichuan gas fields, which currently account for about 55% of output. The Chinese leadership is also counting on an upswing in offshore production. Concerning imports, there are plans to build three LNG import terminals with a view to supplying the Pearl River Delta, the Yangtze River Delta and the Fuijan area respectively, and plans to build pipelines from Yakutsk, Irkutsk and Sakhalin in Russia – and from Turkmenistan and Kazakstan.

In 1995 Japan used about 59 bcm of gas, corresponding to 10–11% of TPES, and imported nearly 100% of supply as LNG. Consumption increased ninefold between 1975 and 1995 but is forecast to grow by only 2–3.7% p.a. between now and 2010. Japan buys gas from the United States and Abu Dhabi in addition to all the Asian gas exporters. Its needs are covered until well into the next century and a number of projects have been identified with a view to extending this period of balance between contracted supply and forecast demand. Japan is aiming for further import diversification, and Qatar and other Middle Eastern countries launching themselves as LNG exporters have obtained contracts with Japanese utilities. The Japanese authorities' interest in the Turkmenistan–China–Japan pipeline project is probably real enough but an expression of their long-term thinking about security of supply rather than a declaration of intent to support such a project in the near future. Imports of Russian gas via pipeline is another longer-term option.

Central Asian gas exports to China could also be economically feasible, according to the World Bank study on gas trade in Asia and the Middle East referred to earlier.[44] Transport costs for moving 27–28 bcm a year via a 6,000 km pipeline to consumption centres in eastern China are put at $106 per 1,000 cu.m, whereas Chinese power producers are paying a price for coal equivalent to $120 per 1,000 cu.m of gas. However, margins after adding production and transportation costs would be slim and the competitiveness of Central Asian gas in any case seems doubtful. Transporting Middle Eastern gas as LNG around India and Malaysia to

---

[44] Kubota (1996).

China would be even more costly than piping Central Asian gas across to the same destinations, but shipping Indonesian, Malaysian and other Southeast Asian gas as LNG to China would cost about the same, and gas could be piped from eastern Siberia to eastern China at a cost of only $57 per 1,000 cu.m.

Summary

Adding up forecast demand in all the markets that in principle could import Caspian gas yields an impressive figure. Western, central and eastern Europe might use more then 600 bcm a year by 2010, against 420 bcm in 1995. Projections of Turkey's gas needs by 2010 range, as noted, from 12 to 60 bcm a year, with the Turkish Ministry of Energy and Natural Resources' expectation of around 30 bcm a year representing the middle ground. Consumption in Pakistan and India could increase from 37 to 120 bcm a year, in China from 17 to 80 bcm a year, and in Japan from about 60 to 80–100 bcm a year between 1995 and 2010. Finally, Ukrainian gas demand is projected to grow by 50% to some 110 bcm. Taken together these markets are seen as expanding from about 615 bcm to more than one trillion cubic metres. Moreover Russia and Iran might want to import gas for optimization purposes. Surely Central Asian gas exporters could ultimately supply up to one-quarter of incremental demand, if the geopolitical and infrastructural conditions fall into place?

From projected needs, however, contracted volumes should be subtracted. As noted, west European needs seem fully covered at least until 2005. The central and east European countries are only just beginning to import gas under regular long-term contracts, but agreements and ongoing negotiations with Gazprom indicate that Russia will remain their key, if not sole, foreign supplier. Turkey appears to have signed enough memoranda of understanding and letters of intent with exporters other than Central Asian ones to meet its supply needs for decades ahead. The other non-FSU markets are covered by contracts and agreements to a lesser extent, but they are also more difficult to access for distance and geopolitical reasons.

Apart from the fact that only a small share of European gas demand up to 2010 remains to be covered, it should be considered that an established supplier to a particular market generally has an easier job than a new supplier landing new contracts in that market, except when buyers aim specifically for further import diversification; and that an established exporter with a good track record would probably be preferred to a new, untried exporter by an importing country even in the absence of any previous contact between the established exporter and the importer. Thus, the chances of Caspian gas producers being chosen to fill remaining supply–demand gaps would depend on the level of competition in individual markets. In the next chapter we look at the competitors to the Caspian states – their reserves, current positions, ambitions and strategies.

6 COMPETITORS

Established competitors in western Europe

Norway, Netherlands, United Kingdom

Norway, the Netherlands and the United Kingdom between them hold 86% of western Europe's proven gas reserves and in 1995 accounted for 76% of its gas production. The three countries are at different stages of maturity as gas producers: whereas Norway's reserves of 3,000 bcm and 1995 output of 32 bcm yield an r/p ratio of almost 95 years, the Netherlands' reserves of 1,815 bcm and production of 78.4 bcm, and the UK's 700 bcm and 76 bcm, imply r/p ratios of 23 years and 9 years respectively.

Norway's existing contracts stipulate an increase in exports to 70–75 bcm a year by 2005, and if opportunities arise, output could be increased considerably beyond this level. Norway is counting on extensions of current contracts with Germany, France, the Netherlands, Belgium, Austria, Spain, Italy and – since March 1997 – the Czech Republic. It is concerned about whether and how sales could be increased without triggering gas-to-gas competition and provoking calls for price discounts, and would like to resume exports to the United Kingdom. Norwegian gas sellers also hope to further strengthen Norway's position in southern Europe and gain shares of the central and east European markets. Especially in the latter they could in the future compete with Central Asia.

Dutch gas production is kept in line with domestic demand and exports. The Dutch gas market is close to saturation while at the same time Gasunie – the company in charge of imports, exports and transmission – is restricted in its pursuit of export contracts, and hence output has for years fluctuated around a flat trend. Recently the huge Groningen field – the backbone of the Dutch gas industry which is used to balance supply and demand – has shown signs of depletion, and Gasunie's position as western Europe's swing producer could become difficult to sustain. The Dutch authorities have responded by lifting restrictions on E&D in environmentally sensitive areas and improving licensing terms, and in a recent White Paper on energy policy it is proposed to give Gasunie more freedom to position itself as a gas trader. The company has already moved towards a more aggressive export strategy: in 1996 it formed a strategic alliance with Gazprom whereby Gasunie will contract with central and east European countries striving for a diversification of imports, Gazprom will deliver the gas physically but the Dutch company will guarantee deliveries from Groningen. Although Dutch hopes of landing a contract along these lines with the Czech Republic were frustrated, other buyers could find the offer of relatively cheap Russian gas coming with a Dutch guarantee irresistible.

UK gas production, which some years ago was thought to be on the brink of decline, increased by more than 50% between 1990 and 1995, and the level of activity of the UK continental shelf illustrates how misleading r/p ratios can be as a production forecasting tool. The UK, which until now has produced gas only for domestic consumption, may in the near future join the ranks of Europe's gas exporters; the Interconnector pipeline between Bacton and Zeebrugge is scheduled for completion in 1998 and will be able to move 20 bcm a year from the UK to the Continent and 9 bcm a year in the opposite direction.

Russia

With more than one-third of the world's proven gas reserves, and accounting in 1995 for more than a quarter of world gas production and almost half of world gas exports,[45] Russia (represented by Gazprom) has so much market power in the CIS and east and central European gas markets that entry conditions for other producers/exporters range from difficult to hopeless. Gazprom is also a strong player in western Europe and could become one in key Asian markets.

Russia is more than a competitor to the Caspian area gas producers and hopeful exporters in that to some extent Moscow also plays the role of referee. Competitiveness in terms of costs, gas reserves, track record as producer-exporter, financial strength and technical and managerial resources may count for little if the playing field is not level, and that is certainly the case if one competitor has the political means to put the others out of the race. That does not mean, however, that Gazprom would not have been able to hold on to – and possibly enlarge – its export market shares even in the absence of Russian political influence in the Caspian area.

Gazprom's finances do not mirror the company's strong position in terms of gas reserves, output and exports, and its standing with high-ranking Russian politicians. By April 1997 Gazprom was owed a total of 69.5 trillion roubles by Russian industry and other gas consumers, and in turn had debts of 20 trillion roubles to the federal budget. Moreover, payment problems were reportedly escalating rather than being brought under control.

---

[45] Including Russian exports to the other FSU republics.

In this situation Gazprom badly needs to further strengthen its positions in solvent markets. The company intends to boost deliveries to Europe by 50 bcm a year, i.e., to some 170 bcm a year, over the next few years. Such a growth in exports would require additional pipeline capacity, and Gazprom is implementing two major transportation projects: the building of the so-called Yamal pipeline initially from the Nadym-Purtaz region across Russia, Belarus and Poland to western Europe, and the building of new pipelines via Moldova, Romania and Bulgaria to southeast Europe. The latter project would strengthen Gazprom's hold on markets of prime interest to the Caucasian and Central Asian gas producers. The Russian company is also apparently thinking about accessing Turkey via a subsea pipeline across the Black Sea, but water depths of up to 2,000 m along the route spell major engineering challenges and high costs; the idea may have been put forward mainly to put pressure on recalcitrant parties to other projects.

Positioning itself to capture a high share of incremental demand, Gazprom has set up trading houses in European states buying Russian gas. Recently some of them have actively tried to take over import contracts and explored possibilities for engaging in direct sales to industry and power plants and spot sales. None of the Caspian area gas producers have the resources to prepare for future market share battles in this way.

Gazprom's targets for Asia are perhaps less precisely stated, but in 1996 it joined the consortium which hopes to construct a pipeline from Turkmenistan via Afghanistan to Pakistan, and the company also sees China as a possible market for east Siberian gas and is taking positions in projects to build pipelines from the FSU area to southwest Asia. Since 1994 Russian and Chinese experts have been working on a scheme to build one or more large gas pipelines from fields northwest of Lake Baikal across Russia and China to the Yellow Sea, and in 1996 President Yeltsin and his Chinese counterpart, President Jiang Zemin, signed an agreement providing for the completion of feasibility studies within two years, and an intergovernmental agreement on building a gas pipeline with a capacity of at least 20 bcm a year from an as yet unnamed field in eastern Siberia via Mongolia to China. This project could be seen as a competitor to the Turkmenistan–China–Japan project, pointing China in the direction of an alternative gas supply strategy.

There is speculation that Gazprom could become a more cooperative animal, perhaps even split into many companies of which one could sell transportation services on a commercial basis to foreign as well as Russian gas producers, thus normalizing the playing field. However, such a reform seems many years away. The Russian government is under strong pressure from the International Monetary Fund and other international financial institutions to rein in the monopolies supplying network-bound energy, i.e., the UES (Unified Energy System) and Gazprom, and

First Deputy Prime Minister Boris Nemtsov tried during the spring of 1997 to reassert the government's role in running Gazprom by calling for a reallocation of the responsibility for managing the state's shares in the company from the company itself to the state. Other reforms put on the agenda were the introduction of a single transport tariff for all gas producers and competition for rights to exploit new reserves. Industrial lobbies and the State Duma protested, however, and Nemtsov was forced to offer reassurance that no one wanted to break up Gazprom.

Algeria

Algeria is the biggest gas producer among the Mediterranean littoral states and also in OPEC, despite the fact that other members have much more gas. Proven reserves are estimated at about 3,700 bcm. Gross production in 1995 was 136.1 bcm, but almost half of this was reinjected and close to 10% flared, vented or lost, leaving marketed output at 58.1 bcm. The r/p ratio was about 53 years; 65% of output – 37.5 bcm – was exported, primarily to Italy, France, Spain and Belgium.

Social, religious and political unrest hangs over petroleum activities in Algeria, and the south European countries receiving Algerian gas via the Transmed and Maghreb–Europe pipelines, or as LNG, have taken care to diversify their imports.[46] However, the Algerian authorities have so far managed to protect the oil and gas fields in the desert south of the country and the pipelines running northward to the coast, northwestward to Tunisia and northeastward to Morocco. The Islamic opposition has neither the resources nor the organization to mount massive attacks on these installations.

In 1996 Sonatrach, the Algerian state oil and gas company, entered into a combined E&P and gas marketing deal with BP. The UK heavyweight will develop known fields and look for as yet unknown ones in an area southwest of the key Hassi R'Mel field with a view to exporting the output to southern Europe. The deal was hailed as an important testimony both to foreign companies' willingness to invest in Algeria in spite of tensions, and to Algeria's increasing pragmatism in its dealings with foreign companies. It could both directly and indirectly contribute to saving the country from falling behind in the struggle for positions in the European gas market.

Sonatrach has high hopes for the future, expecting to increase gas exports to around 60 bcm a year in the medium term and possibly 100 bcm a year in the long term. Exports will be half and half piped gas and LNG. Pipelines appear not to be a

---

[46] Portugal depends for its gas supply entirely on Algerian imports, but gas is a new fuel and will for some time remain a marginal fuel for the Portuguese, leaving security of supply issues manageable. In the longer run Portugal plans to supplement its Algerian gas supply with LNG imported from other sources.

problem – the capacity of the Transmed line to Italy can by the addition of two compressor stations be raised from 24 to 30 bcm a year, and that of the Maghreb–Europe line to Spain can in a similar way be increased from 8.5 to 18.5 bcm a year.

Barring a serious turn for the worse in domestic political life, Algeria looks set to remain a strong competitor especially in the south European gas markets. Transportation distances are short and Sonatrach has gained a reputation for efficiency and aggressiveness. Central Asia is already facing Algerian competition in the Turkish market, and could do so almost anywhere it tries to secure contracts in Europe.

New competitors in Europe and elsewhere

Iran

As noted, northern Iran looks set to become a market for Turkmen gas. Also, Iran looks likely to become a partner to Turkmenistan in Ashgabat's plans to sell gas to Turkey and possibly other European countries. However, the dominant feature of Iran's relations to the Central Asian gas producers and exporters could in the longer run be that of a strong competitor in both western and southern export markets.

At 21,000 bcm, Iran's proven gas reserves are truly gigantic. North America's 6,500 bcm and western Europe's 6,400 bcm pale in comparison. Only Russia among the world's nations can boast even larger gas endowments.

In 1978 Iran's gross gas production was about 55 bcm, but the revolution and the outbreak of war between Iran and Iraq caused it to plummet to a low of 16 bcm in 1981. However, the war years saw a gradual recovery, which strengthened in the postwar period; in 1995 gross output came to 75.5 bcm, and by early 1997 annualized output was reported at 81 bcm. This growth notwithstanding, Iran remains a gas producer of the same fairly modest size as the Netherlands and the United Kingdom. The republic's gas r/p ratio is about 260 years. Although such ratios are incomplete guides to what output could and should be, clearly Iran's gas resources remain underutilized.

In 1992 the Iranian government announced a 20-year gas development programme intended to take production to 310 bcm a year. Exports were expected to grow to about 50 bcm a year primarily on the basis of a project to sell gas to Turkey and other European countries via the new pipeline running from northwestern Iran to eastern Turkey, and another project to sell gas to Asia via a pipeline to be built either along the continental shelf of Iran and Pakistan, or overland via Pakistan to India. According to recent speeches by Iranian leaders, this vision is alive and well; exports are now forecast to be in the range of 40–45 bcm a year as early as 2005.

The only export contract signed to date is the one with Turkey. Reportedly, the planning and financing of a 270 km pipeline from Tabriz to the Iranian–Turkish border is proceeding on schedule, and in January 1997 the Turkish authorities asked for bids for the construction of a 300 km pipeline from the border to the Erzurum region. The Iran–Pakistan–India project remains blocked by Pakistani–Indian relations; India wants neither to be at the end of a pipeline controlled by Pakistan nor to contribute to the Pakistani economy through transit tariff payments.

For well-known reasons, the Iranian authorities have a hard time funding E&P and pipeline projects. Foreign companies show up at Iranian presentations and willingly enter into project talks, but few seem in a hurry to get down to business. It may therefore take Iran longer to establish itself as a significant gas exporter than the Iranians themselves profess to believe. However, as and when conditions for Iranian gas exports improve, other Caspian gas producers may be edged out of key markets by their southern neighbour. The current spirit of cooperation between Iran and Turkmenistan could easily come unstuck; after all, the two states are the Middle East/Central Asia region's biggest gas producers and have their eye on the same export markets. Since Iran will control the flow of Turkmen gas across Iranian territory to Turkey, it seems a plausible longer-term scenario that Iran would reserve the bulk of exports in that direction for itself, forcing the Turkmens to try to resuscitate trans-Caspian pipeline plans or concentrate on other markets.

Middle Eastern and African competitors

Qatar's gas reserves are estimated at 7,100 bcm. The bulk of reserves are located in the offshore North field, the world's largest non-associated gas field. It is being developed in stages by various consortia of companies. Qatargas, which includes Total, Mobil, Mitsui and Marubeni in addition to the Qatari government, will produce LNG for exports to Japan. Rasgas, a JV between Mobil and the government, will supply LNG to South Korea, Thailand, Taiwan, China, India and Turkey. A third LNG project driven by Enron and directed at the Israeli, Jordanian, Italian and Indian markets has been delayed as the partners have failed to secure the necessary sales agreements.

If only the Qatargas and Rasgas projects are implemented on schedule, Qatar could by 2000 be producing about 42 bcm of gas per year and exporting 22 bcm as LNG. Meanwhile, the so-called Gulf South Asia Gas Project sponsored by various foreign companies is trying to drum up interest in building a pipeline capable of exporting 20 bcm a year from the North field to Pakistan with an overland segment across the UAE and an offshore segment along the Iranian coast.

Abu Dhabi has proven gas reserves of 5,380 bcm. LNG exports in 1995 amounted to 6.8 bcm, and customers include Belgium, France and Spain in addition to Japan.

Oman's proven gas reserves are minor compared with those of Qatar and Abu Dhabi. Nonetheless, the Omanis see themselves as future exporters of LNG and maybe also piped gas. With respect to LNG, in October 1996 Oman signed an agreement with the Korea Gas Corporation on delivery of the LNG equivalent of 5.7 bcm of gas a year for 25 years, starting in 2000, and negotiations with the Petroleum Authority of Thailand on delivery of 3 bcm a year are at an advanced stage. As for piped gas, the governments of Oman and India in 1993 signed a memorandum of understanding on building a gas export pipeline with a capacity of 10–20 bcm a year from the former state to the latter. Such a pipeline might not interfere directly with Turkmenistan's vision of exporting gas to Pakistan, but could – as a first gas link between the Gulf and the Indian subcontinent – impact on perceptions of the longer-term competitiveness of Central Asian gas in southwest Asian markets. Water depths along the 1,150 km route are up to 3,500 m, calling for as yet untested and expensive technology, and by 1997 the Omani authorities appeared to be losing faith in the project. India, however, refuses to take the Omanis' tentative no for an answer, requesting them instead to examine the possibility of sourcing gas from Abu Dhabi and other neighbours as a supplement to their own reserves. So, the verdict on the level of competition Caspian area gas exporters are likely to face from Oman is still undecided.

Libya exported only 1.5 bcm of gas in 1995, in the form of LNG to Spain, but could soon become a more significant competitor in European and possibly other markets. In 1996 the Libyan government and Agip agreed to build a pipeline from Libya across the Mediterranean to Sicily and onward to the Italian mainland. Exports of about 8 bcm a year via this line could have materialized as early as 2000. With proven reserves of more than 1,300 bcm, Libya certainly has the geological potential to increase exports to this level and beyond. As an LNG exporter, Libya has been hampered by the absence of a liquefied petroleum gas extraction unit at its old liquefaction plant at Marsa el-Brega, which has meant that customers have had to fraction the product. However, the plant is being upgraded and equipped to deliver normal LNG corresponding to 4.5 bcm of gas a year, holding out the possibility of increased LNG exports too.

Egypt does not yet export any gas, but after a series of discoveries off the Nile delta and in the Western Desert, proven reserves are now reported at 850 bcm, the r/p ratio is approaching 60 years, and export schemes abound. The Egyptian authorities and foreign companies holding development rights in the country have for years targeted the Israeli market and pushed a plan to build a pipeline to Israel and onward to Lebanon, Syria and Turkey. The idea thrived on the Israeli–Palestinian peace process; its promoters cleverly started talking about the 'peace pipeline'. They counted their chickens before they were hatched, however; the scheme lost much of its shine after the election of Benjamin Netanyahu as Prime Minister of Israel, the onset of violent clashes between Palestinians and Israeli troops and an Arab League decision to suspend normalization of relations with Israel. Other companies wanting instead to build a gas liquefaction plant near Port Said and export LNG directly to Turkey gradually gained the upper hand, and in 1996 these interests and Botas signed a memorandum of understanding on a build-up of LNG exports to 10 bcm a year from the turn of the century. The originators of the peace pipeline concept responded by proposing to scrap the peace but retain the pipeline; that is, to build a subsea pipeline from Port Said to Iskanderun on the Turkish Mediterranean coast. However, by the spring of 1997 the LNG alternative seemed to have gained the lead.

Nigeria's proven gas reserves are of the same order of magnitude as those of Norway and the UK taken together, i.e., around 3,500 bcm. Nigerian LNG has been expected on the market for years if not decades, but owing – among other things – to the terms offered by the Nigerian government and financial hurdles related to the state of the Nigerian economy, it took a consortium of foreign and Nigerian companies until late 1995 to decide to go ahead with the building of a two-train plant on Bonny Island. Construction began in early 1996 and production is scheduled to start in 1999. The company set up to implement the project has supply agreements with Turkey and other states.

Asian competitors

Asian gas exports are mainly of LNG. Among the exporters of relevance to the Central Asian states' future as gas exporters, **Indonesia** stands out. It supplies 40% of Japan's gas needs and more than three-quarters of those of Korea and Taiwan. The outlook for Indonesia's LNG exports – whether they will increase, remain at today's level or decline – could impact significantly on Japan's and Korea's interest in projects to make Central Asian gas available to East Asia.

Indonesia's proven gas reserves of 3,520 bcm and 1996 production (net of reinjection) of 69.4 bcm provide for a comfortable r/p ratio of 50 years, but key producing fields are in decline and untapped reserves are located far from existing infrastructure. Nonetheless, Indonesia aims to extend all its long-term LNG contracts and to participate in the supply of new markets, thus defending its share of world LNG trade, in the belief that various large development projects – in particular the giant Natuna project – will be implemented on schedule and deliver according to expectations. Whether things will proceed smoothly enough to prevent any doubts about Indonesia's future supply capability remains to be seen.

Malaysia, Brunei and **Australia** are the other significant Asian and Australasian gas producers and LNG exporters. Their combined proven reserves amount to almost 6,000 bcm, their combined gas output in 1995 was 67 bcm and their combined LNG exports that year were 31.2 bcm. Customers are Japan, South Korea, Taiwan and Singapore. The exporters all have some spare capacity, and Australia and Malaysia have projects under evaluation that could further increase gas production and LNG supply.

Summary

The Caspian countries can export their gas in any direction. They will meet formidable competition whatever markets they target. Currently the northern option, including exports to Russia and via Russia to Ukraine, may be defined only by these countries' gas needs and indigenous gas production, but as and when Ukraine's payment problems abate, Gazprom may want to supply an increasing share of its needs and other exporters may descend on Kiev in crowds.

To the west lie Turkey, Israel and eastern, central and western Europe, and here competition is hotting up. The future crucial issue for Turkey appears to be which of the signed memoranda of understanding and letters of intention will lead to contracts and which will lead nowhere. The east and central European states have been captive Gazprom markets and will probably remain dependent on Russia for a high share of gas supplies, but other exporters – especially those that are established in west European markets – are knocking increasingly hard on their doors, trying to exploit their desire for some measure of import diversification.

Western Europe traditionally consumes Dutch, Norwegian, Russian and Algerian gas in addition to indigenous production, and three of these suppliers aim at increasing their market shares. The United Kingdom could become a gas exporter following the commissioning of the Interconnector between Bacton and Zeebrugge. Meanwhile, budding Middle Eastern gas exporters and a string of LNG producers are waiting in the wings, noting that although supply under existing contracts and eventual extensions of existing contracts could exceed demand for some time to come, the structure of the European gas market is under pressure so that opportunities could arise for sales directly to power plants and large end-users and/or into spot markets.

Pursuing the southern option of exports to Pakistan and eventually India, the Caspian states will meet competition from Iran, the Middle Eastern producers and Russia. Iran shares a border with Pakistan and the Middle Eastern producers at least have the advantage of not needing to route their gas via Afghanistan.

The eastern option, i.e., exporting to China, eventually Japan and possibly other East Asian states, will imply challenging a string of established LNG suppliers and, again, Russia, some of whose reserves are located nearer to Chinese consumption centres than are Central Asia's reserves, and which could export gas via pipelines to northern Japan.

So what do these observations on markets and competitors tell us about the prospects for exports of Caspian gas in the order of 90 bcm a year by the year 2010? My extremely tentative conclusion is that if Russian demand for Caspian gas is factored into the equation, a target of 90 bcm a year could be within reach whereas if Russian demand fails to materialize, things could become difficult (see my estimates in Table 10).

Table 10: Caspian gas exports scenario, 2010

Market	Volume (bcm)
Ukraine	25
Turkey	8
Western Europe	9
Central and eastern Europe	5
Pakistan	15
India	5
Iran	5
Russia	20
Total	92

These figures are not, it should be emphasized, the outcome of complex calculations, they are merely guesstimates intended as points of departure for further discussion. It is assumed – for the sake of argument – that one major pipeline project, namely the one to Pakistan, will go ahead, and that some exports onward to India are arranged. A pipeline link to Europe via Turkey is perhaps likely to be realized at an earlier stage, but it is harder to see the Turkish and European markets absorbing the quantities of Caspian gas needed to make the equation come out than it is to see southern Asia doing so. It is assumed that Caspian producers will supply only a modest share of incremental demand in Europe, most likely via existing pipelines. Deliveries of Turkmen gas to northern Iran could make economic sense, although such a trade could be sensitive to whether Iranian deliveries to Turkey increase to envisaged levels, which seems far from assured. Ukraine is seen as remaining a key market. Russian demand is, as noted, the big question mark, derived as it is from an assumption of a certain strategy on the part of Gazprom managers.

In our scenario, Turkmenistan accounts for the bulk of Caspian gas exports over the next 13 years. If Kazak production increases to 24 bcm a year by 2010 and domestic consumption grows according to the assumptions presented above, the country, which today is a net gas importer, will by 2010 be a net gas exporter, but only of some 5 bcm a year. These exports will presumably go to Russia or via Russia to Europe. Uzbekistan's net gas exports are assumed to increase to around 13 bcm a year, but some of this gas will stay within the region as it is assumed that Uzbekistan will continue supplying Kyrgyzstan and Tajikistan; the rest could, for instance, go to Ukraine. Owing to rapid growth in associated gas production, Azerbaijan becomes a net gas exporter to Georgia and Turkey to the tune of 3–4 bcm a year at the end of the forecast period. The scenario assumes that Turkmenistan remains the key supplier of gas to the other South Caucasian republics, and that Turkmen exports to these states and to Turkey, Iran, Europe, Asia, Ukraine and Russia will amount to around 75 bcm a year by 2010.

Again, these figures are merely the results of some juggling around with assumptions and should not be taken too seriously. If Karachaganak takes off against a background of little or no domestic pipeline construction, Kazak gas exports could grow faster. If Shah Deniz comes onstream as quickly as feasible and the export infrastructure is put in place, Azerbaijan could by 2010 be much more than self-sufficient in gas. If these things happen and if the capacity of markets to absorb Caspian gas does not increase correspondingly, Turkmenistan would have to yield market share to its neighbours. Even though 2010 is drawing close and lead times are long in the gas business, any number of scenarios for intra- and extra-regional gas flows in 2010 could be constructed. And if one adopts a longer-term perspective, the range of possibilities widens dramatically. There are good reasons to believe that by 2020, for instance, Kazakstan and perhaps Azerbaijan will account for significantly higher shares of total Caspian gas exports.

7 EXPORT PIPELINE PROJECTS

As noted, the Turkmen authorities reduced gas production by between one-half and two-thirds between 1991 and 1995 because they were refused access to Russian export pipelines to solvent markets and did not have alternative outlets, and for the same reason Kazakstan's Karachaganak field has deteriorated instead of being further developed. It is, perhaps, a facile observation on a highly complex problem that the presence of comparatively low-cost gas reserves on the one hand, and solvent foreign markets on the other, does not automatically generate the infrastructural conditions for exports to get started. Caspian gas production remains limited by FSU demand minus the sum of Russian supply and non-Russian, non-Caspian indigenous production because of a murky web of Russian political designs, Gazprom commercial designs, political unrest inside and around the borders of the FSU and domestic factors such as unstable tax and other investment conditions. How quickly pipelines would be built and exports increase if these problems melted away is, of course, highly uncertain; as noted, Caspian gas does not seem to be the cheapest alternative either to western Europe or to Asian markets.

A number of gas export pipeline projects are being pursued, and while some appear to be little more than declarations of intent or vain wishes for the distant future, others enjoy the support of governments and international companies alike and could be realized if political framework conditions improve. Often it is hard not only to evaluate the chances of a project going ahead on the assumption that the memoranda of understanding and agreements underpinning it can be taken at face value, but also to form an opinion on the real short-term and longer-term agendas of the parties involved. Governments may issue declarations on projects with other governments for purely political reasons, and companies may offer their support in order to look good in governmental eyes knowing that they may never have to act on their words.

Below we outline some of the export routes and pipeline projects for Caspian gas that have been proposed since the break-up of the FSU. Unsurprisingly, most of them originate from the cramped position of the Turkmen gas industry since the early 1990s.

Turkmenistan–Turkey–Europe

The Turkmen authorities have for almost four years promoted the construction of a gas export pipeline from Turkmenistan to Turkey to sell gas to that country and gain access to markets further west via Turkish pipelines. The route to Turkey has at times seemed debatable, with third parties arguing the merits of building the line across the Caspian Sea to Azerbaijan and onward via Georgia to eastern Turkey. The Niyazov administration has, however, stood by its original idea of routing the line south of the Caspian – i.e., via Iran.

In late 1993 Turkmenistan hired a US firm to form a consortium of private companies with the purpose of building and operating a gas export pipeline system from Turkmenistan to Turkey. At the same time an interstate Council of Ministers was formed under the leadership of President Niyazov and including the energy ministers of Russia, Kazakstan, Iran, Turkey and Turkmenistan,[47] to direct the activities of the consortium. This concept survived until late 1994 when it was decided that the Turkmen government, and not private interests, should own the pipeline, and that a new joint stock company, Turkmenistan Transcontinental Gas Pipeline (TTGP), should be established to plan, finance, construct and operate it.

The project was to be carried out in two stages. Initially, a system with a capacity of 15 bcm a year would be built with a view to supplying the Turkish market. Under an agreement signed by President Niyazov and President Demirel in October 1994, exports to Turkey were to start at 2 bcm in 1998 and increase in steps to 15 bcm a year from 2010. In time, the capacity of the system would be increased to 28 bcm a year with a view to supplying markets further west.

The pipeline would start at the Korpedzhe gas field in western Turkmenistan. Reserves in that region were thought to be large enough to support production of as much gas as would be needed during the line's projected 30-year lifetime. Eventually, additional gas could be sourced from fields in the Amu Darya basin in eastern Turkmenistan.

From Korpedzhe the pipeline would run southward to the Turkmen–Iranian border and then curve around the Elburz mountains and Tehran before turning northwestward and running to Dogubayazit near the Iranian–Turkish border. Transportation onward to Turkish and European consumers would be the responsibility of the purchasers. The total length of the line would be about 1,500 km, of which about 10% would be on Turkmen territory and the rest on Iranian territory. With a diameter of 1,420 mm and equipped with five compressor stations in addition to the gas receiving and compression plant at Korpedzhe, it would be able to move about 15 bcm a year, i.e., as much gas as Turkey had agreed to buy. With another five compressor stations capacity would increase to 28 bcm a year.

---

[47]In January 1995 Ukraine also joined the Council.

Investment costs of putting in place a system with a capacity of 15 bcm a year were estimated at about $2.75 billion. Increasing the capacity to 28 bcm a year would require an additional $1 billion. Pipeline investments in Turkmenistan would amount to about $225 million, and investments in gas production, gathering and processing to $300–500 million.[48]

Getting the project started has been an uphill struggle for the Turkmen government. The main problem was, and is, that US sanctions against Iran make international financial institutions and private lenders reluctant to commit sums to schemes involving Iran. However, the prospects for the project received a boost in July 1997, when the US government stated that a Turkmenistan–Iran–Turkey gas line would not fall foul of its economic sanctions, on the grounds that the principal beneficiaries would be Turkmenistan and Turkey, not Iran. Mobilizing equity has been difficult too, as the Turkmen and Iranian economies are both in bad shape. Possibly because the project has seemed so unlikely to take off, Russia has maintained a low profile on its implementation; otherwise, the Russians might have seen their economic and geopolitical interests threatened.

However, the basic idea of supplying Turkmen gas to Turkey and possibly other European countries via Iran is alive and well. It is now being pursued in a modular way through the construction of a 200 km pipeline, of 12 bcm a year capacity, from Korpedzhe to Kurt-Kui in northeast Iran where it will link up with an existing east–west transmission pipeline running from the Khangiran field to Tabriz in northwest Iran; a 270 km line from Tabriz to Dogubeyazit; a 300 km line from the border to Erzurum in Turkey; and finally an 800 km line from Erzurum to Ankara. The latter pipelines will carry also – or primarily – Iranian gas to Turkey under the agreement signed in 1996. The cost of building the Korpedzhe-Kurt-Kui line is put at $190 million. Initially it will carry 2 bcm a year of Turkmen gas to the Neka power station in northern Iran. Early in the next century deliveries will supposedly reach 10 bcm a year. An affiliate of the National Iranian Oil Company is building the line, which is scheduled for completion in late 1997. Ashgabat will pay for the portion on Turkmen territory – 90% in gas deliveries over three years and 10% in cash.

At the same time both public and private interests are looking into other options. Bowing to the inevitability of continuing to work with Russia and Gazprom, President Niyazov has signed a gas trade memorandum of understanding with President Demirel whereby Turkmenistan is to export to Turkey 2 bcm a year in 1998, 5 bcm a year from 1999 to 2004, 10 bcm a year in 2005–9 and 15 bcm a year

---

[48] Estimates of the costs of building a pipeline from the Iranian–Turkish border to the Turkish–Bulgarian border with a capacity corresponding to Turkey's needs and the planned exports to Europe of up to 13 bcm range from $3.25 billion to $5.25 billion.

in 2010–20; initially this would flow through existing pipelines running via Kazakstan, Russia and Georgia to Armenia, from where a short pipeline would have to be built to Turkey. As a longer-term solution, this route suffers from the fact that Gazprom also plans to enter the Balkans through the Caucasus, leaving the junior partner in a vulnerable position. President Niyazov may reason, however, that playing on many horses simultaneously increases the chances of winning.

As noted, third parties – namely the US company Oil Capital and Botas – have proposed to construct a gas pipeline from Turkmenbashi (formerly Krasnovodsk) on the Turkmen Caspian Sea coast across the sea to Azerbaijan and onward to Georgia and Turkey, making use of an existing 720 mm gas pipeline originating at the Oil Rocks field offshore Azerbaijan and running via Baku, Kazi Magomed, Mingechaur and Akstafa to the Azeri–Georgian border and onward via Tbilisi to Kutaisi in western Georgia. From there it would be necessary to build a new 300 km pipeline to the Georgian–Turkish border and onward to Trabzon on the Turkish Black Sea coast. The proposed gasline would run parallel to AIOC's 'early oil' pipeline terminating at Supsa, holding out possibilities for the common use of installations and reduced costs.

Turkmenistan–Pakistan

In August 1993 Turkmenistan's President Niyazov and Pakistan's Prime Minister Benazir Bhutto signed a memorandum of understanding on building a gas export pipeline with a capacity of about 20 bcm a year from Turkmenistan through Afghanistan to Pakistan. A year and a half elapsed without action, but in mid-March 1995 the memorandum was revived and a pre-feasibility study announced. Turkmenistan and Pakistan would set up a company to float international tenders and arrange financing. It appeared that the Bridas Corporation – an Argentinian company involved in a joint venture with Turkmen interests developing various Turkmen oil fields – and a group of Japanese companies would be involved in the project. Bridas reportedly offered to put up part of the equity. In May 1995 President Niyazov and Prime Minister Chernomyrdin agreed that Gazprom should be part of the consortium building the pipeline. The Turkmen government has also officially invited India to join the project, holding out the possibility of extending the line to northern Indian markets and increasing its capacity to 40 bcm a year.

The line, which would have a diameter of 510 mm, would run from Yashlar, a large Turkmen gas field – reserves are put at almost 800 bcm – scheduled for development by a joint venture between Bridas and the Turkmen government, through western Afghanistan to Chaman on the Afghan–Pakistani border, onward to the provincial capital of Quetta and finally to Baluchistan in western Pakistan where the country's main gas fields are located. There it would link up with Pakistani gas trunk pipelines. The length of the line would be around 1,400 km. Construction costs were estimated at about \$3 billion.

By October 1995, however, the Bridas project appeared to have fallen from grace as a consortium of Unocal Corp. and Delta Oil Company signed a contract with the Turkmen government on building and operating a 1,464-km pipeline with a diameter of 1,220 mm from the Dauletabad field to Multan in northern Pakistan. The capacity of the line would be similar to that of the planned Bridas line. Construction costs were estimated at \$1.9 billion. Extending the line 640 km to a terminal near Delhi in India would cost an additional \$600 million. The consortium agreed to take delivery of 20 bcm a year at the Turkmen–Afghan border for 35 years and market it in Asia at its own risk. Unocal and Delta hope to establish a strong presence in the Pakistani energy sector – they also plan to construct an oil pipeline from Chardzou in Turkmenistan to Gwadar on the Pakistani Arabian Sea coast, and to build and operate gas-fired power plants in Pakistan.

The Russian authorities reacted calmly to the intrusion of new players on the Turkmen gas scene, perhaps assuming that the Unocal/Delta team would be stuck with the Afghanistan problem and viewing the signing of the contract as a political move intended to strengthen the bargaining positions of both sides *vis-à-vis* other interests rather than as an economic accord. Turkmenistan is negotiating with Russia on access to Gazprom's pipelines, and could perhaps get a better deal if it appeared to be on the verge of acquiring alternative outlets for its gas. Turkmenistan could also receive more foreign investment if it is seen to be handling its partnership with Unocal and Delta well. The two companies could gain access to E&P ventures in Turkmenistan in return for their manifest willingness to work with the government – whether the project takes off or not.

Later Unocal/Delta statements and moves indicate that the companies are serious about the project, but have no fresh ideas on how to deal with the extreme social and political instability of Afghanistan. Unocal representatives indicate that the company is prepared to wait for at least 2–3 years for conditions to improve to the point where construction can commence. The Taliban movement's takeover of Kabul in 1996 was seen as an encouraging development for the project. Later indications that the civil war could continue and that Afghanistan could remain without a central government controlling the entire country were evidently disappointing, as were various statements and actions by the Taliban indicating that they could be difficult and internationally embarrassing partners.

Bridas meanwhile has taken Unocal to court for 'tortuous interference' in its plan to export Yashlar gas to Pakistan, and claims that the plan is still on. Unocal and Delta are waiting for the fog surrounding power relationships in Afghanistan to clear; Bridas has opened an office in Kabul and claims to have secured the support of the Taliban – which needs money now – in addition to foreign finance for its project. Bridas has also filed complaints against the Turkmen government with the Paris International Chamber of Commerce for illegal interference with a Bridas-operated joint venture's oil exports, and seems to many observers to have cut itself off from further pursuing its pipeline project. However, President Niyazov too needs money now, and could at the end of the day decide to let bygones be bygones and reward Bridas for its aggressiveness.

Turkmenistan–China–Japan

In April 1994 Turkmenistan and China signed a protocol of intent to build a gas pipeline from Central Asia to the east coast of China and onward to Japan. According to the Turkmen authorities, the Mitsubishi Corporation, the Chinese National Petroleum Corporation and other firms were sufficiently interested in the project to be willing to finance it. In reality the companies were interested in looking into the project. During 1995 Exxon joined them to carry out a feasibility study. The US company is developing fields in the Chinese Xinjiang province and could eventually become a user of the line.

The pipeline would start at the Turkmen–Uzbek border near Khiva, traverse Uzbekistan and Kazakstan (whose governments have approved of the project) before entering China and skirting the Tarim basin on its way to the Yellow Sea, implying possibilities for cooperation on moving not only Turkmen, but also Chinese gas to markets.[49] There would be a need for at least 16 compressor stations along the route – reported to be around 6,500 km – to move 28 bcm a year, which is the envisaged level of Turkmen gas exports to the Far East.

How to transport gas not consumed in China on to Japan remains to be decided. One possibility would be to build a liquefaction plant at Lianyungang on the East China Sea and have LNG tankers shuttle between this facility and a regasification plant in Japan. Another possibility would be to extend the pipeline across the sea – some 900 km – and land the gas in the vicinity of Nagasaki on the island of Kyushu.

The whole system would take at least 4–5 years to build. Preliminarily costs have been put at about $12 billion. This sum would pay for a 1,440 mm pipeline, compressor stations to provide for a capacity of 30 bcm a year, and a liquefaction plant with a capacity of 10 million tonnes a year..[50]

The main problems with the Turkmenistan–China–Japan projects are the size of the task of building a 6–7,000 km pipeline; the costs; the political, legal and other

[49] See Paik (1997).
[50] Recently, the Turkmen authorities have put costs at $9.5 billion. Presumably, this estimate refers only to the pipeline and the necessary compressor stations, not to the envisaged liquefaction facilities on the Yellow Sea coast.

complexities raised by a project involving two, possibly three transit countries; and uncertainty about both the competitiveness of Turkmen gas in East Asian markets at least 4–5 years into the future, and the size of Turkmenistan's gas reserves, which will determine the ability of the Turkmens to supply sufficient gas for as long as necessary to amortize the project, especially in the light of Ashgabat's simultaneous negotiations on other large-scale export pipelines. Most observers see Central Asian gas exports across China as an option only for the second or third decade of the next century. Judging by the relatively low intensity with which Turkmen authorities are promoting this project, they may be operating with a similar time perspective.

Kazakstan–China

The Kazak authorities have proposed to foreign lenders and investors the construction of a 1,200 km pipeline across the country from Atyrau on the Caspian Sea to Kumkol in central Kazakstan, and possibly – at a later stage – onward to eastern Kazakstan and China, with the twin purposes of making Karachaganak gas available to regions which currently have no gas supply and establishing conditions for gas exports to the Far East. Such a project could eliminate Kazakstan's exports to Russia, but it would also put an end to the Western Karachaganak partners' ambitions of exporting the gas to Europe, and has therefore not received much support from its putative funders.

Iran–Armenia, Georgia–Armenia–Turkey

The Caucasian republics also are seething with gas pipeline plans. Armenia, which has suffered badly from its traditional dependence on Azerbaijan as transit country for the bulk of its gas imports and whose sole operating import pipeline via Georgia is exposed to terrorism, has since 1992 been negotiating with Iran on the construction of an import pipeline and imports of some 1.5–1.8 bcm of gas a year. The line would run from Tabriz in Iran to Megri on the Iranian–Armenian border, a distance of 100 km, and thence a further 40 km to Kadjaran in Armenia. With a diameter of 620 mm it would cost an estimated $120 million. Funding problems have kept the idea from realization, however. One plan whereby Armenia would pay for the construction of the line against reimbursement with gas has proved infeasible as neither Iran's participation in the venture nor the state of the Armenian economy has served to attract lenders; another whereby Iran would put up the money has proved equally unrealistic.

Recently, this project appears to have been shelved in favour of a Russian proposal to export gas to Turkey via Georgia and Armenia. In January 1997 Russia and Armenia signed an agreement to form a joint venture with the purpose of (i) upgrading an existing 350-km pipeline from Airum on the Georgian–Armenian border to Gyumri 12 km from the Armenian–Turkish border; (ii) cooperating with Turkish companies on the building of a new 80-km pipeline from Gyumri to Kars in Turkey; and (iii) building a new, bigger line parallel to the existing one from Airum to Gyumri which would take the capacity of the system from 4–5 to 9 bcm a year. Armenia would buy 1 bcm a year from the line and receive another 0.4–0.5 bcm a year as transit fees. However, as noted above in relation to the Turkish gas market, this project seems to be in competition with another Russian scheme to build a sub-sea pipeline from Tuapse to Trabzon. Both these projects, as well as many other schemes to supply the Turkish market, seem to turn on the fulfilment of the Turkish gas industry's extremely optimistic market growth predictions.

8 CONCLUSIONS

From a resource point of view, Turkmenistan has the potential to become an important supplier of gas to parts of Europe and/or Asia, and one or two of the other petroleum-producing Caspian republics also could develop into significant if not world-class gas exporters. Gas resources, however, do not necessarily turn the countries holding them into gas exporters. There need to be markets for the gas, and pipelines linking fields with markets.

Since the Soviet Union ceased to exist and discussions on the Caspian republics' petroleum resources got under way, the absence of export pipelines other than those linking up with Transneft's and Gazprom's lines has seemed to be the binding constraint on exports; and the complex and turbulent politics of the region have seemed the key barrier to constructing new export pipelines circumventing Russian territory.

Politics and perceptions of political risk have certainly complicated the building of both gas and oil pipelines. Relevant aspects of the politics of the area include Russia's viewpoints on its rights and interests in the southern tier of FSU republics, and US attempts to contain Iran, involving threats of sanctions against Western firms investing in Iran and the obligation of US directors of the World Bank and other international financial institutions to vote against projects involving Iran. Political risk means, among other things, the risk of war or civil strife around installations and the risk that host country governments may unilaterally change the rules of the game to the disadvantage of investors. There is no lack of examples of any of these risk factors around the Caspian Sea, the most spectacular example being the high probability of damage to people and installations for anyone venturing into Afghanistan. At a more mundane level, investors still have to cope with weaknesses in legal and tax systems, red tape and slow decision-making in most of the countries in the area.

However, investment decisions depend on perceptions of commercial risks and rewards as well as on evaluations of political risk. And as noted in Chapter 1, here there is an important difference between oil pipeline projects and gas pipeline projects. Oil export pipelines carry oil to terminals from where the whole world can be accessed, or to areas where trade in crude and refined products is developed to such an extent that there is no risk of not finding customers, only a risk of being paid less than expected. Thus, gaining access to oil export pipelines with adequate capacity will allow Azerbaijan and Kazakstan to increase exports as rapidly as the gap between production and domestic consumption can be increased. Gas export pipelines entering Europe and Asia, on the other hand, carry gas to one purchaser or a handful of buyers along the pipeline route, implying that if these buyers do not want the gas after all, it would be awkward, even if at all possible, to take it elsewhere. In fact, if the gas is not already sold, the pipeline probably will not be built.

Even if the existing political and infrastructural constraints on Caspian gas exports were removed – for instance, if the Russian authorities announced the availability (against payment of world-level transportation tariffs, of course) of as much space in their export pipelines as the Caspian producers required – the latter might easily find customers for small amounts of gas outside the FSU, but might face a lengthy battle trying to secure major sales.

In western Europe they would have to compete for contracts stipulating delivery start-up in perhaps ten years' time, and approach customers with better offers than those of established and experienced suppliers, and of an army of other new, low-cost suppliers. The notion that Europe needs Caspian gas for security of supply reasons, and therefore should be ready both to help finance the necessary infrastructure and to give Caspian gas some kind of preference, is probably an illusion. And if current long-term contract and pricing arrangements should unravel – a possible scenario in the view of most oil and gas companies active in the European market – it would not necessarily benefit the Caspian producers relative to other producers, many of which are exploiting their current market positions and financial muscle to further tailor their products and services to anticipated customer requirements.

Some central and eastern European countries are carefully trying to diversify gas imports, but are likely to remain heavily dependent on Russian gas, if for no other reason than the near-impossibility for other suppliers to compete with Gazprom on price in this part of the world.

The other markets to which suppliers flock – Turkey and Pakistan, for instance – are exciting because of their potential, not because of the opportunities they represent here and now. And if liberalization should sweep through the European gas market, driving prices down towards supply-cost levels, conceivably competition would harden further in these and other still regulated markets.

In short, even if politics and political risk factors arguably constitute the current binding constraint on Caspian gas exports outside the FSU, commercial constraints lurk just around the corner, and it is possible – although not a foregone conclusion – that at the end of the day these could deal the hardest blows to Caspian producers' visions of becoming major exporters.

Of possible markets for Caspian gas, Russia appears potentially the biggest, though possibly also the most uncertain, as Gazprom would have to adopt one among many feasible strategies if a need for Caspian gas is to arise. Hence the paradoxical situation that while the Caspian republics strive to wrest their gas exports out of Gazprom's grip, their best chances of becoming major exporters may remain in the hands of Moscow.

Ambiguous market signals notwithstanding, the Turkmen government's pursuit of an unambiguously export-oriented gas strategy makes sense. Turkmenistan can produce much more gas than can be utilized at home, and has little else to offer to the world. There is a plan to make gas available to 100% of Turkmen households, but as Turkmenistan's population is about as big as Norway's, even a partial implementation of this plan – full implementation would probably be excessively costly – would not cut too deeply into its export potential. The government's dreams of turning Turkmenistan into a producer/exporter of gas-based petrochemicals are unlikely to receive sufficient external support,[51] despite Japanese companies' reported interest, and the outlook for exports of gas-based electricity is at best uncertain.

Though generally claiming to believe in gas resource estimates that would warrant large-scale exports, other Caspian leaders do not emphasize exports the way Turkmen leaders do. The Nazarbayev administration appears more bent on securing gas for the new capital, Akmola, and other cities outside the areas that can be served by existing transmission pipelines than on joining the ranks of world-class gas exporters. After unsuccessfully trying to persuade the companies developing Karachaganak to build a pipeline and ship gas eastwards to the central parts of the country, the government reportedly made the building of such a pipeline a condition when tendering the responsibility for running the republic's transmission pipeline systems.

The Uzbek leaders are even less upbeat than their Kazak counterparts about their country's chances of becoming a top-division gas exporter; sustained self-sufficiency, not exports, seems the prime gas policy target. As noted, Uzbekistan exports gas to other Central Asian republics, but the political aspects of that trade probably count for more than the economic aspects, and it will hardly ever become big business. Owing to the size of the Uzbek population and the level of gas consumption, even a moderate economic recovery will trigger significant growth in gas use in absolute terms, implying a need to forge ahead with E&P just to prevent, or at least delay, Uzbekistan's becoming a net gas importer.

As for the fourth petroleum-producing Caspian republic, Azerbaijan, even though it already is a net gas importer, the Azeri leaders' ambitions do not stop at self-sufficiency; it is hoped that offshore gas production will allow for small- to medium-scale exports, primarily to Turkey. Although Azeri gas use is currently constrained by

---

[51] 'The world ethylene industry is in the midst of a construction boom. Capacity is expected to peak later this decade, resulting in lower utilization and weak markets.' *Oil & Gas Journal*, 19 May 1997.

supply, implying a high probability of a leap in consumption as and when constraints are lifted, it is not clear that gas use would continue to grow in step with the economy. Azeri heavy industry is generally very inefficient with respect to energy as well as to other inputs, and uncompetitive by international standards, so that even a hesitant adoption of economic stabilization and liberalization policies will force the downsizing or closure of some of the republics' key industrial gas users.

It bears repeating that current resource estimates are uncertain and that there are more examples in the history of petroleum of geologists erring on the conservative side than of the opposite. The Kazak and Azeri sectors of the Caspian Sea, and perhaps other poorly explored areas, could conceivably turn current estimates upside down.

Nonetheless, it seems that while Turkmen gas does matter and will continue to matter to other FSU republics' gas supply, and probably sooner or later will find its way onto world markets and then begin to matter also to some non-FSU countries' supply, as far as the other petroleum-producing Caspian republics are concerned, their gas matters mainly to themselves. This, of course, does not make Caspian gas developments less important to observers interested in the welfare of Caspian populations and the geopolitics of the area. Where the gas share of TPES is high, uninterrupted and unconstrained supply is a key to economic growth, economic independence and social and political stability. Where it is not so high, there may be a potential for substitution from other fuels to gas, possibly freeing up oil for exports and/or contributing to the attainment of environmental goals. Systematic exploitation of local possibilities to create value from gas could at the end of the day prove to be the most rewarding way ahead.

REFERENCES

Azerbaijan International, various editions.

Cedigaz (1996), *Natural Gas in the World 1996 Survey*, Rueil Malmaison.

DRI/McGraw-Hill (1996), *World Energy Series European Outlook*, December 1996 edition, Paris.

East European Markets, various editions.

East–West Executive Guide, various editions.

Eastern Bloc Energy, various editions.

Eastern European Energy Report, various editions.

Economist Intelligence Unit, *Armenia/Georgia/Azerbaijan, Kazakstan* and *Kyrgyz Republic/Tajikistan/Turkmenistan/Uzbekistan Country Profiles* and *Quarterly Reports*, various editions.

European Bank for Reconstruction and Development (1997), *Transition Report*, London.

European Bank for Reconstruction and Development (1997), *Transition Report Update*, London.

European Gas Markets, various editions.

Gas Matters, various editions.

Hammond, John and Yakovlev, Andrei (1996), 'Oil and Gas Projects in Turkmenistan: Structuring Investments', in *Oil & Gas Law and Taxation Review*, August.

International Energy Agency (1995a), *Energy Policies of Ukraine*, OECD, Paris.

International Energy Agency (1997), *Energy Prices and Taxes, Fourth Quarter 1996*, OECD, Paris.

International Energy Agency (1996a), *Energy Statistics and Balances of Non-OECD Countries, 1993-94*, OECD, Paris.

International Energy Agency (1995b), *The IEA Natural Gas Security Study*, OECD, Paris.

International Energy Agency (1996b), *Oil and Gas Information 1995*, OECD, Paris.

International Energy Agency (1996c), *World Energy Outlook 1996*, OECD, Paris.

Kaser, Michael (1997), *The Economies of Kazakstan and Uzbekistan*, Former Soviet South Project Key Paper, RIIA, London.

Kubota, Shigeru (1996), *Natural Gas Trade in Asia and the Middle East*, World Bank

Occasional Paper, Washington, DC.

Nefte Compass, various editions.

OECD, *Short-Term Economic Indicators,* various editions.

Oil & Gas Journal, various editions.

Paik, Keun-Wook (1995), *Gas and Oil in Northeast Asia*, RIIA, London.

Paik, Keun-Wook (1997), *Tarim Basin Energy Development: Implications for Russian and Central Asian Oil and Gas Exports to China,* FSS Briefing No.14, RIIA, London.

Paterson, Dennis (1995), 'Matching Energy and Transportation Needs', conference paper delivered in Istanbul, March.

Petroconsultants, *Foreign Scouting Service – CIS*, various editions.

Petroleum Economist (1995), *Pakistan & Bangladesh: Their Energy Potential.* London.

Petroleum Economist, various editions.

PetroStudies, Co. (1995), *Gas Business in Russia and Other FSU Countries, Vol. 7: Central Asia*, Malmö.

PlanEcon, Inc. (1995), *The Electric Power Industry in Central Asia*, Washington DC.

PlanEcon, Inc., *Energy Outlook for the Former Soviet Republics*, various editions

Pomfret, Richard (1995), *The Economies of Central Asia*, Princeton University Press, New Jersey.

Riva, Joseph P., Jr. (1994), *Petroleum Exploration Opportunities in the Former Soviet Union*, PennWell Books, Tulsa.

Roberts, John (1996), *Caspian Pipelines*, Former Soviet South Project Key Paper, RIIA, London.

Russian Petroleum Investor, various editions.

Stern, Jonathan P (1995), *The Russian Natural Gas 'Bubble': Consequences for European Gas Markets*, RIIA, London.

Stoppard, Michael (1996), *A New Order for Gas in Europe?*, Oxford Institute for Energy Studies, Oxford.

WEFA Energy (1996), *The 1996 European Natural Gas Supply – Demand Report*, London.

Wood Mackenzie (1997), *European Energy Service. Reference Booklet 1997*, Edinburgh.

World Bank (1993), *Azerbaijan Energy Sector Review*, Washington DC.

World Bank (1993), *Kazakstan Energy Sector Review*, Washington DC.

World Bank (1994), *Turkmenistan*, Washington DC.

World Bank (1993), *Uzbekistan: An Agenda for Economic Reform,* Washington DC.

World Bank, *World Development Report*, various editions.

Zviagelskaia, Irina (1995), *The Russian Policy Debate on Central Asia,* Former Soviet South Project Key Paper, RIIA, London.